GUIDING GOD'S CHILDREN

Tolbert McCarroll

Guiding God's Children

**a foundation for spiritual growth
in the home**

paulist press   *new york/ramsey*

Library of Congress
Catalog Card Number: 83-60376

ISBN: 0-8091-2547-1

Published by Paulist Press
545 Island Road, Ramsey, N.J. 07446

Printed and bound in the
United States of America

Contents

Part IV
NEW PATTERNS IN
CHRISTIAN LIVING

APPENDICES

Acknowledgements

The photographs on pages 32 and 172 are by Ann Friedman; one on page ii (forepiece) is by Sister Christine van Swearingen, O.S.U.; those on 8 and 152 are by Sister Michael Marie Zobelein, O.P.; the photograph on page 70 is by Father James Geoghegan, O.C.D.

All scriptural texts are taken from *The Jerusalem Bible,* copyright © 1966, 1967, 1968 by Darton, Longman & Todd, Ltd. and Doubleday & Company, Inc., and used by the kind permission of the publisher. All rights reserved. Quotes from *Sharing the Light of Faith: National Catechetical Directory for Catholics of the United States (NCD),* copyright © 1979, by the United States Catholic Conference, Department of Education, and used with the kind permission of the copyright holder. All rights reserved.

I wish to thank the following publishers for permission graciously given to reprint material from the following copyrighted works. In all cases all rights are reserved.

Addison-Wesley Publishing Co.
  Bob Samples, *The Metaphoric Mind: A Celebration of Creative Consciousness,* copyright © 1976.
George Allen & Unwin Ltd.
  Chogyam Trungpa, Born in Tibet, copyright © 1971.
Cistercian Publications, Inc.
  Thomas Merton, *The Climate of Monastic Prayer,* copyright © 1969.

Crossroad Publishing Co.
Avery Dulles, S.J., *A Church to Believe In,* copyright ©
1982.
Bernard Häring, *Free and Faithful in Christ,* copyright ©
1981.
Karl Rahner, *Concern for the Church,* copyright © 1981.
John A. T. Robinson, *The Roots of a Radical,* copyright ©
1981.
Harper & Row
Abraham H. Maslow, *Motivation and Personality,* 2nd ed.,
copyright © 1970.
Houghton Mifflin Co.
Carl R. Rogers, *On Becoming a Person,* copyright © 1961.
Kappa Delta Pi, an honor society in education
Abraham H. Maslow, *Religions, Values and Peak Experiences,* copyright © 1964.
Macmillan, Inc.
Gordon W. Allport, *The Individual and His Religion: A Psychological Interpretation,* copyright © 1950.
Rabindranath Tagore, *The Religion of Man,* copyright ©
1931.
Naturegraph Publishers, Inc.
David Villasenor, *Tapestries in Sand,* copyright © 1966.
Newman Press
Bernard Häring, *The Law of Christ,* copyright © 1966.
Northwestern University Press
Alfred Adler, *Superiority and Social Interest: A Collection
of Later Writings,* copyright © 1964.
Oxford University Press, Inc.
James Hennesy, S.J., *American Catholics,* copyright © 1981.
Arnold Toynbee, *Experiences,* copyright © 1969.
Paulist Press
Joseph Gelineau, *The Liturgy Today and Tomorrow,* copyright © 1979.
Morton T. Kelsey, *Caring: How Can We Love One Another?* copyright © 1981.
Penguin Books
Matsuo Basho, *The Narrow Road to the Deep North and
Other Travel Sketches,* copyright © 1966.

Charles Scribner's Sons
 Martin Buber, *I and Thou,* copyright © 1970.
Seabury Press, Inc.
 Bernard Lonergan, *Methods in Theology,* copyright ©
 1972.
 John H. Westerhoff, III, *Will Our Children Have Faith?*
 copyright © 1976.
Winston Press
 Richard McBrien, *Catholicism,* copyright © 1981.

 I am also grateful for permission to reprint copyrighted material from *The Journal of Transpersonal Psychology,* in James
Shultz's "Stages on the Spiritual Path, A Buddhist Perspective,"
copyright © 1975.

**dedicated
to
my sister**

Julian De Rossi

**and others like her
who quietly bring
the peace of God
into young lives**

Introduction

This book is written to support those who care enough about the future of humanity to invest in the spiritual growth of our children. In most cases these will be parents. Some have partners, some do not. All are attempting to make a family in the often hostile environment of our materialist society.

Some of the readers are part of the institutional Church and some are not. But all, knowingly or unknowingly, are a part of that mysterious touching between heaven and earth which was uniquely manifested in Jesus Christ, and which continues to exist in the community of pilgrim disciples which we term "the people of God." Those who may feel alienated from the Church in this age may, through their authentic spiritual concerns, be providing the tension in which we will discover more clearly the light of Christ for our age. The offspring of both the comfortable and the uncomfortable members of the Christian community are essential for the evolving story of our people.

I have in mind the particular needs of those who have come from a Christian background, but except for specific examples and some selection in emphasis, what is written can apply to all who are willing to tolerate the vocabulary in which I quest for my own spiritual reality.

This book is also written for the pastors, teachers, and other ministers whose gifts and office make them responsible for laying the foundation of the Church of the future. Certainly the Christian community will never again be a separate ghetto holding out against the secular society. Since the mid-century we have accepted that our place is *in* the world. There is no romantic escape path open to us. The solution to all our problems must be found, to borrow from Albert Camus, "in the wall against which we are living." What we do is no more important than how we do it. We must facilitate a Gospel community which is recreated in each of its facets, one of which is the individual family. Partly because of our mistakes as Church people, today's Christian families are being asked to perform Herculean tasks in forming the next generation of disciples. Unless we give them more support now, there will be no adequate foundation for whatever we hope to build in the future.

A Crossroads

This is not a child care book. It is not another how-to-do-it manual offering simple solutions to problems of raising children. It would not be inaccurate to view this work as a contribution to Christian spirituality, but even that is not the whole picture. There can no longer be an isolated spiritual life. To quest for God is to become involved in God's world. The purpose of prayer, the keystone of spirituality, is not to escape from and deny life but rather to more fully comprehend it and live it. Hopefully this book is a contribution to the growing concern for how we as followers of Christ can touch our world.

The most significant point of common interest between the reader and the author will be simply that we are mutual inhabitants of this earth at this particular moment in history.

Spiritual Hunger

The encounter with God stimulates a disturbing freedom. As religion became increasingly an institutional phenomenon, spirituality became more suspect to the managers of the institution. Generations of Christians were guided to safer and safer spiritual lives, until in the 1950's we found a private, dry, mechanical devotionalism which presented only a plastic menu to alleviate the growing spiritual hunger of the world. Christian spirituality was an embarrassment and ignored in the 1960's. An American Church, already defensive about its prior modest intellectual achievements, and proud of its growing list of academically acceptable leaders, did not wish to be too closely associated with spiritual dimensions which hard-headed rationalists dismiss out of hand as "anti-intellectual." In the 1970's many men and women turned to other sources for spiritual nourishment. At one point both non-Christian spiritual seekers and some radical Christian theologians agreed that the spiritual tradition of Christianity was hopelessly irrelevant and passing from the world scene.

But ordinary women and men know that the hunger persists. Intellectualism is no more satisfying than materialism. Another alternative is evolving. It is coming from the bottom up, from the experience of individual quests. Pent-up spiritual energy is certainly being released. How we will channel this vitality is still unclear.

Purpose and Scheme

This book is written to encourage the view that the spiritual development of young children is at least as significant as any other part of their growth. Today an increasing number of Christian educators are directly or indirectly abandoning their concern for this younger age group. What is presented here is intended to be a support for those parents and others who are frustrated and discouraged by the enormity of their task.

Part I provides an overall framework and presents a brief but hopefully sufficient theoretical base on which the other parts can rest.

Part II explores the process of growth, including spiritual development. It is important to distinguish what is presented here from the customary curriculum and procedure of "religious education." The suggestion is also made that the developmental and neo-Freudian psychological schools on which contemporary religious education largely relies are not the only human development models for spiritual growth. We look at the research on the specialization of the hemispheres of the brain, humanistic psychology, and the experiences of other cultures.

A detailed practical program of twelve steps is contained in Part III. These steps have evolved over the past twenty years and are influenced by Native American culture, the practical aspects of formation in Christian communities which have included children, and the growing body of psychological-spiritual studies resulting from the encounter between Eastern and Western religious experience.

Part IV takes a brief look at emerging new patterns in Christian living. The world in which we guide our children will be different from the world in which they will live as adults. I take as a framework Karl Rahner's recent study of the possible characteristics of the spirituality of the future. These final chapters attempt to relate the specific concerns of the book to the broader challenges of living as Christians in the era which is just dawning.

Although not a professional religious educator, I do recognize that their path intersects with spirituality. Their concerns and contributions are relevant to the issues raised in the following pages. Perhaps also some of the critiques from a Christian educator who is outside the traditional religious education sphere might resonate with the experiences and frustrations of some religious educators today. An attempt to further this dialogue is contained in Appendix B under the title, "Beyond Faith Development: Some Reflections on Religious Education." Appendix A is a sharing with any interested reader of a practical little process which I have used to help in confusing spiritual times.

Perspective and Vocabulary

I am a Catholic monk and one who directs the spiritual formation of others. I have also been a parent to children now grown, and am presently an active godparent to several children. But my primary perspective in writing this book is not from any of these viewpoints.

Basically, I come to the subject as a Christian humanist. What has brought me to these concerns and suggestions is part of a general exploration of what it means to become a person, to attempt to achieve our humanity as part of the reality of life. In this quest I am more comfortable with observable phenomena than general theory. My values are existential in that I am concerned with the individual choices to be made in life and the need for authenticity and freedom. For this freedom to be genuine it must include being free of preoccupation with self and a liberty to commit myself to something other than myself. In this latter task I have found no better assistance than in the life and presence in the world of Jesus Christ. Through this freedom in Christ I am encouraged to attempt that condition which Rahner has described as an "unconditional acceptance of human existence." In the rare moments when I can comprehend that it is part of my essential nature to accept the grace to meet this challenge, I am no longer "monk," "Catholic," "parent," "spiritual director," "humanist," or even "Christian." All facets converge in a simple concern for living. This deep interest binds me to all my fellow pilgrims with whom I share this moment of history. Somehow in the total process we each are found by God more frequently than we lose God.

An attempt has been made to use an inclusive language. However, I balk at artificial contrivances such as "her/his." At times I must run the risk of offending the sensitive reader with traditional vocabulary when I am unable to write naturally otherwise. I accept that God is, as Julian of Norwich suggests, both mother and father, and neither. Nonetheless, I am not aware of a satisfactory alternative to the traditional masculine reference. Whatever the weakness of vocabulary, the point is that spiritual growth itself should be inclusive; no significant distinction should be made between young boys and girls, at least to the extent the subject is explored in these pages.

There is another problem with vocabulary. Theology, spirituality, psychology, anthropology, education and other disciplines touched on in this book can all become elaborate games. Concepts and counter-concepts become only pieces on an intellectual chess board with little real value in life. To counteract this tendency in myself, and perhaps in some of the readers, I have included some pictures of children. The attempt is to use a little "left-hand" (see Chapter 3) balance to help both author and reader remember that we are sharing a concern for real children. I owe a special debt to Ann Friedman, Sister Christine van Swearingen, O.S.U., Sister Michael Marie Zobelein, O.P., and Father James Geoghegan, O.C.D., whose considerable professional talents have provided the photographs.

The overall task of writing was made possible by two members of my own community, Sister Mary Martha and Sister Julian DeRossi, who worked as co-partners at every step.

I also happily acknowledge a debt to all the children who have patiently endured and survived my clumsy experiments in Christian education.

The Diaspora

When I look at the children in my life I see tomorrow's Christians. Some will be certain and sure in their faith; others—I hope—will have doubts. We need both. I believe that in at least one important way all of these children will be closer to understanding Jesus than those in my own generation.

The Christian story began when we were a minority. We were a means by which God could introduce more hope, love, and perhaps faith among all the people. The restrictive concept of "conquering the world for Christ" came not from God but from us. We had taken a wrong turn and viewed God as a super-monarch. Consequently, the Church became a super-state. "Christianity" turned into "Christendom." In the past century we have begun to escape from that mentality. The Second Vatican Council blocked the way back; we cannot return to former times even if we wished to do so. We must now move ahead. We find ourselves walking paths strangely parallel to those of our early Christian mothers and fathers. Then, as now, we wandered in a world which sees us as alien and is nonetheless drawn to the message our lives are supposed to reflect. Again, we can be a spiritual leaven in the world.

Then as now, each of us is not only a *part* of the Christian community, there are times when each of us *is* the community. Sometimes this will occur when we are most uncertain and even alienated from our spiritual heritage. Yet there are times when we know that we are all God has. For those who recognize such a moment when they look into the eyes of a child, this book has been written.

Tolbert McCarroll
Starcross Monastery
Annapolis, California

Part I
RESPONDING
TO LOVE

1. A Special Advent

An important contribution in Zen Buddhism is the thirteenth century document of the Soto school, *Instructions to the Chief Cook.* The kitchen master is told to find the essence of the spiritual life within "a blade of grass." Material for a great sermon comes from "a particle of dust." The cook must "love water and rice as parents love children." A question for today's Christian is: Do we love our children and our religion as much as the Zen cook loved water and rice?

Our Jewish neighbors have always known that love includes a serious obligation to spiritually prepare children for adult life. This high priority of parenthood is beautifully symbolized at the Passover Haggadah, when the youngest child asks the head of the household, "Why is this night different from all other nights?" All the children listen as the tradition of the ages is transmitted, and they grow up knowing that what they are being taught will be passed on to their own children in the years to come.

It is the Western way to put down our great learning in complex thoughts wrapped in heavy books. Yet how we yearn, even hunger, for the simplicity of the Zen cook or the Jewish child who finds theology not in the latest book but in a blade of grass or an obvious question. Our hearts respond when we read that the risen Lord was recognized in Emmaus, not in philosophical argument but at "the breaking of bread" (Lk 24:13–35). The pages which follow will focus on recognizing the risen Lord in other ordinary events of everyday life.

This book is written out of a concern for the future of the world community.

As Christians wishing to explore our role in the scheme of things, we begin not with the Church, or Christ, or even God. We start with what it means to be human. Through our awareness of ourselves and of God we counteract the constant tendency to slip into a banal existence. The Christians' greatest collective sin is encouraging each other to concentrate on the trifles of life. The times when we have been at our best we have encouraged an age to live more fully.

The people of God, including those outside the institutional Church, must face the threat of an age, only one generation away, which will have even less knowledge of the peace of the Gospel than we now possess. Let us review some of the signs of trouble.

The Weakness of Christian Spiritual Formation

A recent survey sponsored by the National Conference of Catholic Bishops accepts the statistic that "forty-two percent of all Catholics drop out sometime during their lives," and many will never return.[1] To put it more bluntly, at least ten and a half million Catholics in the United States today will permanently stop looking to the Catholic Church for their spiritual nourishment. Some of these will feel compelled to make this move precisely because they are good and serious people who believe they must leave in good conscience.

Equally alarming is the fate of those remaining in the Church. The tremendous increase in courses, workshops, books, cassettes, and degree programs concerning spirituality and prayer is a symptom of the spiritually arid condition in much of the Christian community.

A related concern is expressed in recent articles where the future of Church leadership in this country is described as being in "a precariously weakened state." Responsible theologians are predicting a serious leadership void as early as the next decade.[2] The result will be a radical change, not only in who will be allowed to lead, but more fundamentally in regard to what type of leadership is required. There is a growing concern that all who lead must first see themselves as part of a larger group who "minister," which in turn must be part of a much larger group which is trying to lead Christian lives. The demise of professional clericalism is not mourned, but the resulting gap is not being adequately bridged.

The basic hunger of men and women for spiritual nourishment has not lessened. Young people continue to rush to the spiritual teachers of Eastern, near-Eastern, Native American and other non-Christian religious traditions. True, some, like myself, will recognize at some point that as nourishing as our experience has been in the East we must return home to graft our experience onto our own roots. If we do not we will begin to feel as if we are a perpetual tourist. We must come home in order to feel at home. This quandary was put well by a "former" Catholic who had come to the west coast to better experience Zen Buddhism. He was a young and conscientious father who asked the question, "But what will we do on Sundays?" Some, perhaps most, who ask that question will return. But our number is not enough to justify the bromide that "Christians leave the Churches in their teens and return in their thirties." Equally strong evidence points to an increasing number of Americans of every religious background who are comfortably situated among the "no religious preference" category. This number has increased dramatically, some four hundred percent, since 1966. Even many of those who assume the Christian label will view the choice as an entirely personal matter and utterly reject as impossibly frustrating and unproductive any affiliation with a community of fellow Christians.

What is the problem? Why not just let these things happen? My primary concern, as expressed above, arises from an interest in the world, which needs and deserves the best that religion can provide. Secondarily, and more personally, I have been associated with a large number of people who are seriously frustrated in their adult spiritual quests because they have been deprived of an appropriate spiritual formation in their childhood. They live in a painful tension and often find release in non-constructive and shallow experiences. Some are flexible enough to "become as little children again" and to have a new start, even quite late in life. But many are not able to do so, and they continue to build elaborate superstructures without any foundation. Time after time their castles fall down. Sometimes these pilgrims are injured.

Why has Christian spiritual formation failed in so many lives? As long as the pews were filled we did not worry. In the smug triumphalist period we each had our little fortress Church where we gathered and pretended there were no problems. But in fact a trend has slowly progressed through the centuries.

Religious educators insist, and correctly so, that one of the most important problems has been our attempt to teach the wrong thing at the wrong time. There has been too much reliance upon conditioning rather than education. Like Pavlov's dog, the young Christians could salivate catechism answers at the sound of a question, but this was not a skill which helped them in the normal spiritual crises of their adult lives. Too much of Christianity was presented, we are told, in terms of myths, which became confused in children's minds with such things as Easter bunnies and could easily be discarded in adolescence.

Perhaps the most serious problem has been the growing diminution of conscious encounters with God. I have never met any person who did not encounter God at some time. But what is often lacking has been an ongoing experience of spiritual growth. We can observe that children are excited by an occasional reading of a book. But we know that there must be a program by which they continually grow in reading skill if it is to become part of their makeup and to nurture them throughout their lives. We have not maintained a similar sensitivity to the equally necessary spiritual development of our children. Why?

In recent times we have witnessed an increasing problem among the parents and spiritual pastors of our children, who are also having difficulty encountering the Divine. For example, of the more than eight thousand priests who left the active Catholic ministry in the United States in recent years, most had a reasoned public statement which included everything from personal concerns, such as a desire for family life, to stands on principle, such as reactions to excessive authoritarianism. However, many also had a deep private reason which had to do with questions such as: "How can I continue in the pulpit when I do not pray anymore?" It would be irresponsible to suggest that every priest who left felt this way, or that every priest who stayed did not. However, I have had enough dialogues with reflective men in these circumstances to feel safe in generalizing that with them, and undoubtedly with many who stayed, there was a spiritual problem. Has it not also been the same with other leaders, and with many parents?

Somehow in the wisdom that always seems to grace the people of God we are recognizing and beginning to cope with the problem of our own spiritual deficiencies. But in the meantime, what do we do about our children? Parents are confused and often feel inadequate. The tendency is to send the children off to weekly Confraternity of Christian Doctrine classes, Sunday school, or a local parochial school. But spiritual formation cannot adequately be taught in a classroom. A teacher can do no more than support the process. The home is the only place for spiritual growth during the early years of life.

This book is written for those seriously concerned parents and "foster godparents" (see Chapter 7) who are willing to invest in the spiritual growth of their children between birth and adolescence. What follows is an attempt to assist those who are willing to make a major contribution to our children's future and the future of the world. Admittedly, this may be only a minority of parents and godparents, as is often asserted. But it is from this minority that the future Christian leaders and many of the future fulfilled human beings of this world are going to come. At this moment some future Pope is having his or her tummy tickled by a loving and concerned parent. And even more important, some time today a future Francis, Benedict or Teresa may run toward you with a dirty face and a big smile.

This book is also written for teachers and pastors and other ministers who are willing to support parents in this tremendous undertaking. The families need training, assistance, encouragement and affirmation. While recognizing the family as the "principal school," Vatican II nonetheless reminds us that "the Church as a mother is under an obligation" to assist in the education of Christian children.[3] It is not enough to discharge that obligation by attempting to turn the whole problem over to professional religious educators.

If my assumptions about the seriousness of the problem are

correct, or even if they might be correct, then there is a major danger to the future of the Christian message to the world. Does it matter? When Michael Ramsey retired as archbishop of Canterbury in 1974 he was asked during a BBC interview to name the greatest change during his tenure as leader of the Anglican community. His response surprised many. Without hesitation, but with sorrow, Dr. Ramsey pointed to the rapid increase of selfishness in the world.[4] This scholarly Christian leader named a central problem of our age. The past events of this century lead us to expect that various secular alternatives, including communism, nationalism and individualism, will not turn the tide toward a more caring community. The Gospel alternative is yet to be seriously proposed except in small corners of the Christian community and the world. If the Christian counter-balance to a "me first" world is to be put forward in the future we must turn our attention now to the spiritual formation of today's young children. In this task the gifts of all of our leaders are urgently needed. We are becoming increasingly proficient at throwing our head back and proclaiming the theological relevance of Christianity to the major social and philosophical issues of our day. But we must also be willing to point our head downward. We must, in effect, be willing to develop a waist-high theology that will benefit the younger brothers and sisters of our Christian family. I have no concern for the talent available. I am only apprehensive about the application of that talent.

God's Children

As a last preliminary question let us ask, "Whose children are we talking about?" In North America we have a great possessiveness about our children. At the same time we can ignore many of their basic needs. We consider children "our kids" like any other possession. We often look to them for the satisfaction of our own needs. We act as if they belong to us. It is important for Christians to realize that their children are not private possessions. The children belong to God; we are but the guardians of the children in our care.

Our attitude is symbolically demonstrated in the way we care for infants. Babies in our Western world are carried close to the breast with their faces turned so that generally they see only their mother or father. Many infants in Native American cultures were carried on their mother's back. They faced out to the world. It was not a frightening world because they could feel the mother's back as they walked along. As the Indian mother worked at the necessary requirements of life she would hang the cradleboard up in a tree. There in the soft caressing of the wind, much like the mother's walk, the baby would learn to be at home with the family and with nature. As one Indian sand painter has said:

> The baby is usually placed facing toward the family group, where the "Rock-a-Bye-Baby on the Treetop" would be part of the relationship of the wind, the birds, the tree, the fire, and the home.
>
> The Indian Mother, knowing that she is but the vehicle through which the new soul manifests, faces her child away from her where he may become acquainted with his Maker, while yet feeling the nearness, the rhythm and the love of Mother.[5]

The Modern Family

The model of the family presented in these pages tends to be from a young child's point of view. Children have little concern for the findings of sociologists and psychologists, much less the abstractions of Church or secular law. To the child the family consists of those people with whom you share the dinner table. To the adults in the family, life can be much more complex.

Theologians have gone far in recent years in helping us understand the potential beauty and significance of married life, which enables husbands and wives to be open to the mystery of God. "Marriage," said Vatican II, "involves the good of the whole person." But Church people have lagged behind in comprehending the complex social and personal conditions which often interfere with this idyllic view becoming a reality.

St. Paul reminds husbands and wives: "God has called you to a life of peace" (1 Cor 7:10–16). Unfortunately, many have found little nourishment or peace in a former marriage. As a result, they are raising children as single parents or in a new marital relation which may or may not have the Church's blessing.

These people stand in between the traditional "nuclear" family of the late nineteenth century and the pleasure-oriented advocates of the so-called "post nuclear" era. Many readers could be termed "neo-nuclear" parents. They recognize the value of a stable family life with a father, a mother and children. On the other hand they also recognize, often from bitter personal experience, that a wedding ceremony does not guarantee a healthy family environment.

Sociologically, much of our family life has been based on the fulfillment of needs which are now, for better or worse, being satisfied outside the family situation. One unconscious use of many first marriages is to provide an avenue for independence for the bride or groom. This results in such a limited and romantic horizon that the marriage is often a nullity, even under strict Church law. Consequently, the grace-filled family life is increasingly found in a second relationship.

There are about ten million households in the country where at least one partner has been in a previous marital relationship. In over half of these the partners brought children from the prior marriages. It is estimated that soon half of the children in America will have lived with a single parent at least for several months.

There even seems to be developing a new family situation which researchers term the "bi-nuclear" family. These informal groupings are composed of the present family and various former partners and siblings. The divorces have usually been friendly and child custody is joint. There are regular contacts between the former spouses to discuss issues in their "parallel parenting." The adults are attempting to raise the child in several homes. However, from the child's perspective he or she may be without any home at all.

In addition to the broad spectrum of possible marital arrangements, we must also consider the divergent views on how parents relate to children. First, there is the option to have children. Many simply decide against it, usually because it would interfere with their life-style. This can include everyone from high-swinging pleasure-seekers to celibate clergy. With the advent of some priests and nuns adopting children, it can be said that even celibates who live without children have chosen to do so. The same can be said of some wealthy families whose absentee parenting consists primarily of selecting proper nurses, governesses, camps, prep schools and colleges.

Among those who do choose to raise children there is still a wide difference of approach. On the one hand are those who see having children as an obligation and who are prepared to sacrifice their own life, often with serious psychological results. At the other extreme we see children in some "me generation" homes being treated as romantic inconveniences, rather like a pet cat or dog. In between are the parents who take seriously the task of raising their children and also developing themselves. These often do not receive the support they need. Many a husband still considers a wife's child care activity as of secondary importance to his occupational or recreational interests. The Church, and especially celibate clergy and religious, frequently acts as if raising a child were an automatic affair, rather like growing a tomato. Everyone complains when the process breaks down, but few want to be involved in the details of that process.

Families of Caring Disciples

In all our modern books on family life nothing can be found which will bring greater fulfillment or happiness than the model for Christian family life found in the fundamental teaching and life-style of Jesus of Nazareth. The keystone is mutual care, and there can be no substitute.

The greatest failure of modern Christian life is in loving those who love us. After forty years as a pastor, teacher and counselor, Morton Kelsey has come to this conclusion:

> Few people live satisfactory lives, have satisfactory homes and marriages or make satisfactory relationships with others. . . . If there was one point at which Jesus may have underestimated human frailty, it may have been in his failure to see the difficulties his followers might have in their intimate relationships.[6]

If we wish to guide God's children we must provide a home environment that resembles a Gospel community. What does that imply? Let us begin by taking a look at Jesus' basic attitude. The primary thing he was proclaiming was the coming of the kingdom of God. Into a land of gloom came a great light. It was not a territory or a social order. Rather, a cold uncaring history was being fundamentally altered. God was to be King, the same God who was also our loving Father. In his own time and way God would be manifest in history for our benefit. Our loneliness was at an end, for God had drawn near and peace would replace our anxiety. It would indeed be a world in which:

> The wolf lives with the lamb.
> The panther lies down with the kid.
> Calf and lion cub feed together
> With a little child to lead them (Is 11:6).

This was indeed "good news" (Gospel), but how was it all to come about? In the story of the temptation of Christ by the devil (Mt 4:1–11; Lk 4:1–13) we get some sense of how it will not happen: (1) Stones will not become bread, for "man does not live by bread alone." (2) People cannot put "God to the test" with expectations of great unnatural miracles. (3) Temporal power over "all the kingdoms of the world" is also not to be the answer. In other words, the kingdom of God was not to be brought about by an exclusively economic, occult or political agenda. How, then, was it to come?

> The kingdom of God does not admit of observation, and there will be no one to say, "Look here!" "Look there!" for, you must know, "the kingdom of God is *among you*" (Lk 17:20).

We, with God's help, are to bring about the longed-for peaceful kingdom. Our primary task is to become fully human. This we do, as Karl Rahner has taught, by being a human being whose depths are divine.[7]

In order to show us how this was done, our triumphant

Messiah, our great Savior came not in the form of a supernatural being but as a humble working man. He was a fellow human being who demonstrated by his own life, death and resurrection that salvation was to be sought not outside our daily sorrows and joys, but in their very midst. He was not less human than most of us. He was more human. How do we become fully human? Through love.

> You must love the Lord your God with all your heart, with all your soul, with all your strength and all your mind, and your neighbor as yourself (Lk 10:27–28).

We show this love by caring for and healing each other. We are to forgive each other and be reconciled one to another. Christianity, therefore, assumes community. And the family is the primary level of community life. In Jesus' life-style, his way, his Tao, we find even more practical ways of making loving (Gospel) communities. Jesus accepted suffering and trouble. Life was not assumed to be all rainbows and butterflies. Although a person meek and mild, he walked with the crude, the simple, the blunt, the hot-headed, the sinner. Therefore, community is possible, even with spiritually underdeveloped people.

How did Jesus act in the great chaos of human existence? He was gentle; he did not judge; he reached out for the outcast. To him all were equal in worth—including women and children. He cared for those in need. Yet he was not saccharine; rather he was fully authentic and refused to accept the psychological projections of his disciples:

> Get behind me, Satan! You are an obstacle in my path, because the way you think is not God's way but man's (Mt 16:23).

But even when these corrective slaps of reality came, the hand of brotherhood was never withdrawn. There was no sarcasm, no ridicule, no exclusion.

Who can help comparing our own blundering family experiments with the foregoing examples of community life around Jesus? Let us not lose heart. The essential issue is not

"Do we have a fully Christian family life?" but rather "Are we *attempting* to make our family a Gospel community?" If we are, we have already offered to our children an appropriate environment for spiritual growth. After all, Jesus did not come to congratulate the successful but to encourage the struggling:

> It is not the healthy who need the doctor, but the sick. I did not come to call the virtuous but sinners (Mk 2:17).

The Third Millennium

Christianity is at an important moment in its history. We are only a few years away from beginning the third thousand years. It is more than just a symbol. Karl Rahner has recently observed that the Church itself is changing from a Western institution basically identified with European culture into a world Church. In past years, he tells us, we emphasized uniformity rather than unity. Now in this world Church we are going to have as much of a change as when in the first generation, following Jesus, we changed from an exclusively Jewish Church to one which responded to the whole people of the world, Jew and Gentile.[8]

The future of this third millennium is in our hands today. The new Church which Rahner describes is, in my opinion, not only a community which will include third world cultures; it must also include those within Western culture who have explored counter-cultural approaches to life. It must be a Church which encompasses all those spiritually and religiously minded people who have questioned the traditional beliefs and practices of Christianity. It must be a truly universal experience. And this will require a unique leadership.

In his first encyclical, Pope John Paul II referred to the time before the third millennium as a "special Advent." "We also are in a certain way," he wrote, "in a season of a new Advent, a season of expectation."[9]

This is an image which we ought to keep before us as we explore the issues in this book. There will definitely be a new manifestation of the incarnational mystery by which God touches our world. We are in an Advent, but it is not a passive Advent. This is a time that requires our active reflection and labor.

Somehow we must encourage each other to act as if the very next child we meet will become a spiritual leader who could influence the quality of life in the world to come. And we must also act as if we somehow can do something to assist that child in his or her future work. Both assumptions are probably correct.

Our children desperately need us and we need them.

2. Head Words and Heart Words

Life is a uniform process. Unnecessary distinctions hamper that unity. However, the life process has many facets, and the confusion of one aspect with another can make growth difficult. What follows in this chapter is an attempt to describe some of the facets before we consider the actual process of spiritual growth and how it applies to young people.

A major theme of this book is that the cognitive aspects of formation that is "religious" have been overemphasized, often to the exclusion of the "spiritual" side. This chapter attempts an overview which includes both the intellectual considerations, the "head words" and the more intuitive concerns, that is, various "heart words." This is not simply a matter of style. Increasingly we are coming to realize that a multiple approach to the important issues of life is required because of the basic makeup of our personalities. This will be explored from a psychological point of view in the next section. First, however, let us construct a simple framework on which to hang later ideas. Like any analysis, all of these distinctions are in a sense artificial and may be discarded as soon as they have helped us arrive at a basic orientation.

Appreciating Karl Rahner's warning that there is in theology a danger of "too much scholarship for its own sake" which does not proceed from "the depths of our experience,"[1] my purpose here is to present concepts like "faith," "religion" and "spirituality" in a common sense fashion as an exploration of what is and what is not basic to the spiritual formation of young children.

1. *Our starting point is FAITH, which is a personal knowledge of divine love.*

Faith is "God's love flooding our hearts."[2] *Christian faith* is a personal knowledge of that divine love as disclosed in the life of Jesus Christ. Faith is not primarily a rational process, although it is consistent with our rational faculties. Chinese religious terminology urges us to "think with the heart." It is in this sense that we can speak of "personal knowledge of divine love." We cannot truly define the term "divine love"; neither are we sure about what Jesus disclosed during his life. But it does not matter. Faith exists on a deep level which transcends our intellectual, and indeed our emotional, concerns. Faith is, therefore, not synonymous with "belief," and is to be distinguished from dogmas and other intellectual constructions. Faith is much more significant, for it has to do with the nature of our existence. Our Christian faith is the realization that we are, in some way, in solidarity with the quest of Jesus of Nazareth as he sought to disclose the kingdom of heaven and the love that exists in it.

2. *THEOLOGY is, as St. Anselm and others have said, "Faith seeking understanding."*

The awareness of divine love naturally makes us wish to comprehend it, and our attempt to do so becomes one of our intellectual responses to faith. Theology has been defined as "the study which, through participation in and reflection upon religious faith, seeks to express the content of this faith in the clearest and most coherent language available."[3] In other words theology begins with faith (it should not be simply an academic exercise) and ends with a well-communicated statement (it is not a private reflection). Even though we use our individual intellects, theology is a communal response to faith.

3. *HOPE is an existential[4] response to faith.*

When our heart responds to the awareness of the divine love we take our whole being to God. We are the same persons we were before we experienced faith; we have the same life to live. Faith awakens the hope that we can truly find fulfillment in life. In traditional language, this is a longing for "salvation." In a contemporary phrase of Bernard Lonergan, we are using faith to "resist decay."[5] The decaying process is a perpetual threat to us throughout our lives. As we age we must be sure that we are "still bearing fruit when we are old, still full of sap, still green" (Psalm 91/92). When we stop growing we are subject to all the decay of our environment.

Hope could be termed "faith seeking freedom." Faith arouses a hope for authentic existence, or, more plainly put, a good and meaningful life. Once hope is alive within us, we hungrily approach the Gospel message, the good news, of Jesus Christ.[6] At first we look for personal satisfaction and individual salvation.[7] But soon we discover that our hopes cannot be pursued in a strictly private and personal way. Part of the good news requires us to accept the fact that human life is a sacrament—a visible sign of God's invisible presence. Everything around us can disclose God's love and can be an instrument of the good news. Our ultimate freedom is therefore available to us in encounter with our fellow human beings, the natural world, our history, and all the aspects of the life experience.[8] So, as with the intellectual response to faith (theology), our existential response (hope) cannot be entirely individual and personal but also requires a human solidarity. If we are to realize our hope it must be in contact with the life around us.[9]

Let us pause in this discussion to see where we are in a schematic and simplified way.

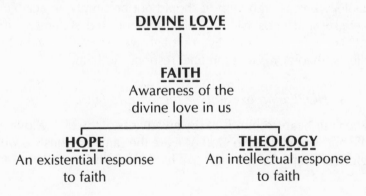

DIVINE LOVE
|
FAITH
Awareness of the
divine love in us

HOPE   **THEOLOGY**
An existential response   An intellectual response
to faith   to faith

4. *RELIGION is the objective facet of hope; SPIRITUAL-ITY is a corresponding subjective facet.*

Spirituality is characterized by (but is not exclusively) a tendency toward a direct encounter with God. The religious facet, on the other hand, seeks God (although not exclusively) through the persons and events of our moment in history. Both the religious and the spiritual facets of hope are fulfilled in the process of everyday living.

In many ways the subjective and objective distinction is arbitrary, and furthermore cannot be fully explored until the concepts in the next chapter on "the left-hand" approach to education have been presented. I nonetheless suggest that we view "religion" as a basically objective response and "spirituality" as a basically subjective response. Perhaps the most classical distinction is found in Luke's story of Mary and Martha:

> In the course of their journey he came to a village, and a woman named Martha welcomed him into her house. She had a sister named Mary, who sat down at the Lord's feet and listened to him speaking. Now Martha, who was distracted with all the serving, said, "Lord, do you not care that my sister is leaving me to do the serving all by myself? Please tell her to help me." But the Lord answered. "Martha, Martha," he said, "you worry and fret about so many things, and yet few are needed, indeed only one. It is Mary who has chosen the better part; it is not to be taken from her" (Lk 10:38–42).

Religion is the Martha of our life. Spirituality is the Mary. On the one hand we are doing God's work, and letting God work in us on the other. St. Teresa of Avila has properly pointed out that, in order to make a true home for the Lord, Mary and Martha must be combined in us in some way. In both dimensions God can and hopefully will be encountered. If we, like Martha, work to create an environment in which we can receive God there is every reason to believe that we will be successful. Spirituality goes somewhat more directly to the source, in a process which is summed up in the Book of Exodus: "Yahweh would speak with Moses face to face, as a man speaks with his friend" (33:11).[10]

Let us now extend our diagram another level.

DIVINE LOVE

FAITH
Awareness of the
divine love in us

HOPE
An existential response
to faith

THEOLOGY
An intellectual response
to faith

SPIRITUALITY
The subjective
facet

RELIGION
The objective
facet

To be more accurate the diagram would have dotted lines connecting "theology" with both "spirituality" and "religion." In order that there be wholeness in the process there must be complete interaction.

5. *RELIGIOUS EDUCATION is the training process for the religious facet of hope.*

In the religious aspect we emphasize such concerns as community[11] and service.[12] When we think of a period of formation and training we are mainly concerned with what is sometimes termed nowadays the "fundamental option," that is, our basic attitude toward life. We attempt to develop in our children a personality that will encourage them to live in accordance with the Gospel message, especially as it relates to our living together as brothers and sisters. We teach common terms, prayers and concepts. Children are trained not only to live in a Christian community but also to explore how that community, and each of us individually, can bear witness to the good news in the larger world. In the field of religious education today we are especially cautious about what is called "faith development," that is, the process by which the religious dimension should be advanced progressively through the various stages of human growth. One popular theory has it that we start from the self-centered approach of the child (desire for reward or fear of punishment) and supposedly move toward the mature religion of later life (embracing faith for faith's sake alone). This theory is critically examined in Appendix B.

6. *SPIRITUAL GROWTH is training in spirituality.*

At the present time spiritual growth should be seen as the story of the practical quests of men and women for freedom through encounter with some kind of nourishing and unchanging stillpoint in the increasingly rapid changing circumstances of our age.

In the past two decades in the United States the tendency in spiritual growth has been toward short term programs in what has been labeled "the mechanics of illumination." This follows on our push-button approach toward human development coming out of the 1960's. There has been a growing emphasis in spiritual circles on technology and methodology to capture the spiritual experience. It is a very American approach to find a solution to a problem by the most direct, and easiest, way possible. The trouble is that we may not have a good grasp of the problem. We can become spiritually trapped in our own gimmicks if they tend to emphasize the individual ego.

At our present juncture in history any consideration of spirituality must revolve around the concept of freedom. For some, the concern has been freedom from environmental factors. Increasingly, however, we are seeking a freedom from that interior problem of our age, extreme individualization. We have been pushed in our experiments with freedom to a sense of aloneness that has become a sickness. Indeed there is an increasing feeling of helplessness about important circumstances surrounding an individual's life. We attempt to solve this soul sickness by obtaining power, money, prestige, sexual prowess and the like. This leads to great mid-life crises when we become aware of the hollowness of our achievements. This period is not infrequently followed by a kind of self-hate which can be projected toward others.

Spiritual growth will vary in the different circumstances of life. For monks and nuns the original formation model in the desert communities of the fourth century was based on athletic training. They were sometimes called the "athletes of God." As a result "asceticism" or spiritual disciplines such as fasting, long prayer, manual labor and spartan living were emphasized. The process was to "renounce" everything but God.

Although spiritual discipline is essential to spiritual growth, we generally agree today that it must be part of a larger picture which enables us to recognize God in our lives. For our young people this awareness is much more important than any external practice.

Let us now complete our diagram:

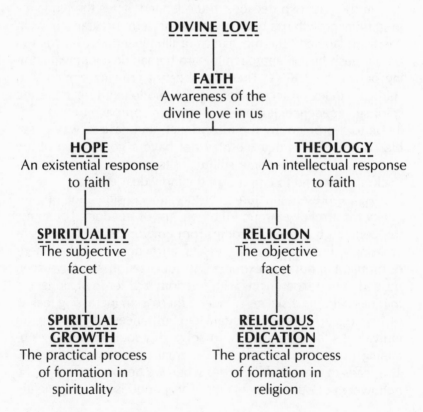

DIVINE LOVE

FAITH
Awareness of the
divine love in us

HOPE
An existential response
to faith

THEOLOGY
An intellectual response
to faith

SPIRITUALITY
The subjective
facet

RELIGION
The objective
facet

**SPIRITUAL
GROWTH**
The practical process
of formation in
spirituality

**RELIGIOUS
EDICATION**
The practical process
of formation in
religion

A Renewed Interest

In the first half of this century the average man or woman in the pew was led to believe that spiritual growth was limited to certain pious devotional practices. As a result the religious education response was greatly overemphasized. If there was anything significant to be found in spirituality it was to be left to an elite. It was, in fact, considered somewhat presumptuous for anyone to attempt to aspire to such heights. Now, since the middle of the century we have had a growing shift in emphasis. Also, we have recognized that Christian spirituality has an actual history which has moved dialectically and has to be interpreted in light of the historical circumstances in which it evolved. Just as with life in general, much of our spiritual life has been in reaction to what has gone immediately before.

The emerging spiritual emphasis at the present time is upon encounter with God in a process which is interrelated with the human sciences, especially psychology.[13] It is within this phenomenon that the concepts in this book have been developed.

There have also been strong forces outside the Christian community which have stimulated the concern for spiritual growth. "New age spirituality" saw people attempting to experience all sorts of imports from around the world. Although this movement is now declining, it still reflects a tremendous spiritual hunger on the part of our people. The institutional Church in the 1960's was simply not ready to broaden its perspective to include these needs. Many who were on these "new" quests had so thoroughly written off the Church that they would not have been impressed with anything coming from that direction anyway. The result has been a certain shallowness. The inner needs of many individuals have not been satisfied and they keep moving from one thing to another. Most people will feel alien when attempting to be filled completely with a spirituality coming from a different cultural background. Some are able to transcend these backgrounds, but most of us are not. As a result we often get into a kind of play-acting syndrome.

Increased attention is being paid to the process by which we can attempt to graft the experience we have gained in various non-Christian spiritualities onto our own cultural roots. The search for these roots may become a significant part of the spiritual history of our age.

Summary

The reason for the distinction between "spiritual growth" and "religious education" is practical. Some time ago in our reaction against simplistic pietism, mechanical methods of prayer and the like, we tended to reject too much of the spiritual dimension. But one of the essential functions of spirituality in our response to faith is to provide for the present experience of God. Therefore, no matter how highly we prize the religious aspect, without a unique sense of God there is an incompleteness that may be fatal to the continuation of the lived-out response to faith. We are left increasingly with the intellectual response of theology, which is not satisfying to the total personality. This is a major weak point in the general development of faith in our age, specifically in regard to our young children.

The dialectic process created a reaction against simplistic devotionalism which led to an overemphasis on religious education (objective) and ignored spiritual growth (subjective). As a result, we failed to gain that freedom from self-interest with which we create the empty space for God, or, more accurately, "the Other," to co-exist in our lives. To satisfy the longing for spirituality young people turned without hesitation to Zen, Yoga, Transcendental Meditation, and other approaches. They felt that these spiritual experiences were quite separate from anything in their own Western cultural heritage.

Now we must synthesize the total process. By an increased emphasis on spiritual growth we can restore a balance to our response to faith. Only when all the facets mentioned in this chapter come together do we fully respond to divine love.

Part II
STAGES
OF GROWTH

3. The Split Brain
and the Tao of Jesus

Spiritual growth begins not in the soul but in the brain, and most specifically, for most people, in the right hemisphere of the brain,[1] which controls and influences the left side of our body and, of course, our left hand. The left hemisphere of the brain performs the same function for the right side and hand.

Ancient lore, especially in the East, recognized important non-rational aspects of the mental process. Consequently, the left hand, from early times, became associated with concepts of the quiet, receptive, mystic, feminine and earthy. In Chinese spirituality this was given the term "Yin." The right hand was active, bright, male, assertive, and associated with expansive heavens. To the Chinese it was known as "Yang." The most significant point regarding Yin and Yang was that they had to fit together. One could not exist without the other. This is demonstrated by the familiar Yin/Yang symbol.

In many religious practices there was a tendency to use the left hand to quiet the active right hand. Because the heart could be perceived on the left hand side of the body, that side was often spoken of as the "heart side." Thinking "with the heart" was contrasted to thinking "with the mind."

We have discovered in this century that there is much more to the left hand/right hand balance than poetic metaphor. Brain research confirms that there are two distinct ways of thinking which must relate uniquely in each person. Gradually we are awakening to the implications of the fact that when this process is not in balance there can be serious consequences.

Left Hemisphere/Right Hemisphere

I prefer to use the older "left hand" and "right hand" phrases. The more correct and contemporary statement would be "right side" and "left side," referring to the two hemispheres of the brain. "Left hand" and "right side" and hemisphere are equivalent terms, as are "right hand" and "left side" and hemisphere.

At this stage of the physical research it is difficult to get precise definitions of the specialization of each hemisphere. Our knowledge has been assisted by intensive studies of stroke victims' brain damage and various experiments with corrective surgery. During the past decade or so the concepts have been introduced into practical learning situations.[2]

It is rather sobering to realize that an entire part of our brain is usually underdeveloped in our educational system. Despite the fact that information on brain hemisphere specialization is generally available, a surprising number of teachers prefer to ignore it. It has been observed that many teachers trained in the rational cognitive approaches to education become uncomfortable when their students explore different mental approaches. In fact, many teachers will do everything they can to encourage students to conform solely to the patterns being presented by the teacher.[3]

Basic Information

Brain damage to left hemisphere (right hand) areas interferes with language facility as well as writing ability and analytical thinking. In general all of our "linear" attitudes, that is, our ability to link things together in sequence, are disturbed. This is always considered "major" damage. It is assumed that a person with left hemisphere damage is no longer able to really function in our society, because this specialization is the aspect of a human being which our society most values. It is the means by which we Western people have civilized the world and developed our technology.

Right hemisphere (left hand) brain damage is not taken so seriously. Furthermore, this damage is more difficult to test. There will, however, be interference with our ability to make music, to draw, and to perceive spatially, and our depth perception is disturbed. These areas are not considered by most people to be as significant as linear functioning.

The hemispheres are linked through the eyes because of a split in the optic nerve, and through a connecting bundle of nerve conduits known as the *corpus callosum.*[4] In infants the two spheres normally function together nicely.[5] The specialization process begins to take place at a later time, and apparently is the result of a process of acculturation. In other words, the way in which we teach our children develops the latent specialization of a brain hemisphere. Our culture's heavy interest in language has led to an early development of the left hemisphere (right hand) side. Western languages are abstract. They must be divided, analyzed and defined. Language skills are an early training ground in practices of logic, order and sequence. As these same processes are emphasized the hemispheric disequilibrium develops. As these left hemisphere functions become more and more culturally valued through the generations there is a tendency to increase the disequilibrium, as has happened in our own culture in the past several hundred years.

Hemispheric Specialization

Let us try a very left-handed (right hemisphere) stab at the special aspects associated with the two hemispheres. This type of definition is speculative and subject to considerable modification depending upon personal life experiences.

LEFT HEMISPHERE (Right Hand)	RIGHT HEMISPHERE (Left Hand)
Sequential	Conceptual
Linear	Cyclical
Logical	Intuitive
Objective	Subjective
Analytic	Wholistic
Dividing	Unifying
Rational	Metaphorical
Vertical thinking	Horizontal thinking
Cognitive	Affective
Intellectual	Creative
Verbal	Spatial
Words	Faces
Active	Receptive/Quiet
Deductive	Imaginative
Accommodation	Assimilation
Literal	Poetic
Abstract sources	Nature sources

The basic distinction is not so much the subjects for specialization but the process. For example language is influenced by both sides, as are words and faces. The importance is how the data are processed—sequentially in the left hemisphere (right hand) and simultaneously in the right hemisphere (left hand).[6] The right hemisphere (left hand) also has a better orientation to space than the left hemisphere (right hand) and is more involved in the process of arts and crafts, music, motion (kinesthetic capabilities) and auditory perception.

It is interesting to compare the effect of strokes on language in different cultures. In the Western world left hemisphere strokes commonly result in a loss of language. There is usually an aphasiac condition in which our ability to read and write is impaired. An interesting phenomenon occurs in Japan where there are two languages. One language, Katakana, closely resembles our own in that it is logical, sequential and has a phonetic relationship between the written character and the sound. This language is increasingly important in Japan's technological society. But there is also an older language, Kanji, which descends from the ancient pictographic Chinese and Japanese languages. Despite centuries of evolution the symbols in Kanji still continue to give no clue to pronunciation and must be viewed in a wholistic way in order to be comprehended. Researchers have found that in Japan left hemisphere strokes will impair Katakana in a quite similar way to impairments in English-speaking countries. However, the stroke victim can still read and write in Kanji.

Non-technical cultures differ radically from us in the equilibrium between the two hemispheres. This gives credence to the contention that the lack of balance is the result of cultural practices. It also suggests the special role that spirituality probably plays in assisting in right hemisphere (left hand) development, as will be explored later.

The hemispheric distinction was simply put by Albert Einstein, who called the intuitive mind (right hemisphere/left hand) a sacred gift and the rational mind (left hemisphere/right hand) a faithful steward. Ironically, however, as we attempt to study and comprehend the genius of Einstein, we reverse the process and make it an almost exclusively left hemisphere (right hand) exercise. Thus in our Western world the faithful servant has become the dominant master. This has occurred not only in the secular domain but also in our responses to faith.

Left-Handed Formation

The right hand/left hand metaphor is of course only a partial truth. Like any tool it can be misapplied and misused. Any analytical description of a wholistic process, such as learning and formation, is going to be inadequate. Nonetheless, this tool is helpful in understanding the basic distinction made in this book between spiritual growth (left hand) and religious education (right hand). To say that spirituality is an entirely left-handed phenomenon or that religion is entirely right-handed is certainly simplistic. Nonetheless, there is importance in recognizing that growth in the spiritual must be through a process which includes left hand education. The failure to recognize this need has resulted in some severe deficiencies in our approach to the training of young Christians.

One difficulty is that right hand (religious education) matters are usually more easily transmitted. Information can be and usually is written down and printed. Left-handed aspects (spiritual growth) are more subtle and often defy words. In one of the left-handed spiritual classics of the East, *The Tao Te Ching,* we learn in the first line:

> The Tao [sacred way] that can be spoken of is not the eternal Tao.
> The name that can be named is not the eternal name.[7]

As a practical help in understanding the different processes between "learning" (religious education) and "the pursuit of the Tao" (spiritual growth) we are instructed in Chapter 48:

> In the pursuit of learning,
>   every day something is added.
> In the pursuit of the Tao
>   every day something is dropped.[8]

The Tao of Jesus

At the time of Jesus religious education concerned laws, practices, moral obligations, Scripture, ritual and other matters which certainly were the type of learning in which "every day something is added." In addition, there was, however, the tradition of the wisdom literature of the Old Testament in which "every day something is dropped." Increasingly, now we find Jesus being presented by scriptural students as a sage of the wisdom tradition.[9]

One of Jesus' most powerful means of teaching seems to have been a dynamic personal contact which challenged the disciple to a radical conversion of life. There was a piercing touching of the heart which cut through many right-handed problems. This is perceived even in the basically rational accounts in the Gospels. The post-Easter account in Luke of the disciples on the road to Emmaus contains a clue of another perception of Jesus. Two demoralized disciples were walking along when Jesus came to them. They did not recognize him. But later while sitting at table they did recognize him in the breaking of the bread.

> Now while he was with them at table, he took the bread and said the blessing; then he broke it and handed it to them. And their eyes were opened and they recognized him (Lk 24:30–31).

Is there a suggestion here that there had been a particularly transcendent association with Jesus at the breaking of bread at previous times? And, if so, is this not one of the explanations that help us better realize the tremendous importance of the Eucharist in the early Church? It was here in this essentially left-handed memorial event that the Christian received significant spiritual formation. Even today, or perhaps especially today, most adults would have to admit to more than occasional questions and doubts about the nature of the Eucharist, but this is usually in cognitive situations while they are contemplating theological niceties concerning such issues as the meaning of the real presence of Christ. However, few have any difficulty in actually participating in a Eucharistic celebration. We may be very worried on our way to the chapel as the right hand suggests that we are preparing to engage in a cultic practice of some sort. However, as we near the tabernacle the left hand helps us to put aside these concerns and respond directly to some kind of presence in the heart.

The Parables

There is an especially intuitive teaching method which has come down to us associated with Jesus—the parables. Here the memory of Jesus is vividly set forth. The Dutch theologian Edward Schillebeeckx has suggested that Jesus was God's own parable to humanity![10]

A parable has been defined as a sort of "kill-joy" statement, an irritant.[11] Its relevance is not obvious and it is a disturbing way of making a point. German scriptural scholars have a saying, "The parable explains but cannot be explained." We cannot control the parable with our rational mind, but we can learn from it with our intuitive gifts. The process has something to do with the recognition of a personal challenge which affects us at a deep level and calls forth some kind of decision. We cannot simply treat the event in an objective and intellectual fashion. We must make an individual response in some way.[12]

Particular parables may well have been used by Jesus in a different fashion than the way in which they were edited and used in the Gospel accounts. Today there is a growing appreciation of the parable as a continuation of the wisdom tradition.[13]

Will We Dance?

Let us take a parable that is found in both Matthew and Luke (Mt 11:16–19; Lk 7:31–35).[14] The more complete Luke version reads:

> What description, then, can I find for the men of this generation? What are they like? They are like children shouting to one another while they sit in the market place:
>
> > "We played the pipes for you,
> > and you wouldn't dance;
> > we sang dirges,
> > and you wouldn't cry."
>
> For John the Baptist comes, not eating bread, not drinking wine, and you say, "He is possessed." The Son of Man comes, eating and drinking, and you say, "Look, a glutton and a drunkard, a friend of tax collectors and sinners." Yet Wisdom has been proved right by all her children.

Basically the parable is used to describe the differences between John the Baptist, who emphasized repentance of sin, and Jesus, who offered a joyful fellowship. But that is not the deep import of the message. For Jesus is speaking to each of his hearers, and to us, by use of the poignant song.

We were presented with two options. We have failed to respond to either. The dirges of John did not call forth our tears. We did not dance to the pipes of Jesus. What then will awaken us to our spiritual hunger?

Another disturbing twist in the parable is that it is the children themselves, those who most want to play, who are chanting this song back and forth. We are like hungry people throwing bread to each other without tasting it. The Anchor Bible translation of the Matthew story suggests that we should hear this parable as Jesus and John calling to the rest of us children. They have presented everything that it is possible to present, and if we children will not respond, then there is a serious issue to be faced.[15] This is reminiscent of Old Testament statements, such as are found in the Book of Ezekiel:

> Son of man, the members of your nation are talking about you on the ramparts and in doorways. They keep saying, "Come and hear the word that has come from Yahweh." They throng toward you; my people sit down in front of you and listen to your words, but they do not act on them. They cannot tell the truth and their hearts are set on dishonest gain. As far as they are concerned, you are like a love song beautifully sung to music. They listen to your words, but no one puts them into practice (Ez 33:30–32).

A deeper, left-handed communication, is contained in the parable's haunting song. The issue is: Will we dance? Will we cry? It is appropriate and significant that Jesus refers to himself, or at least to God, in the last phrase of this parable as "Wisdom," in the fashion that was so popular, not only in Old Testament times but also among the later spiritual scholars, such as the fourteenth century German mystics.

4. Frustrations in Christian Education

Recent reviews of materials used in religious education classes suggest increase in "linguistic fundamentalism" and note a decrease of "right brain (left hand) religious education."[1] Why has the rational and cognitive aspect of Christian formation been so overemphasized in modern times?

The Decline of Spirituality

Our present difficulties may have commenced in the fourth century when the Christian Church became the official religion of the Roman Empire. A minority of concerned men and women fled to the desert. The majority of Christians certainly did lose touch with the intensity of the age of martyrs. By the time of the merger of interest between the barbarian Franks and the Roman Church in the ninth century there was a marked lessening of the democratic and gentle spirituality of the apostolic period. The Church was respected for its supposed supernatural power over human concerns. Occasionally, when this tendency went to extremes, popular religion moved to the occult, and priests became shamans. During the medieval period, spirituality existed primarily in monasteries and small communities. The majority of Christendom was content, as Meister Eckhart put it in the fourteenth century, to "love God just as they love a cow . . . for the sake of its milk and cheese."[2]

The Reformation and Counter-Reformation made great demands upon proper thinking and correct formulation. There is nothing like an inquisition to turn a person into a proper-thinking (right-handed) Christian. However, other factors were also at work at this time. Increased literacy and the availability of books written in the vernacular made religious concepts more available to ordinary people. These concepts were generally abstractions. There was and still is a tendency for teachers not to differentiate between their own ability to think in the abstract and the ability they require of their students. Consequently, children tend to be taught religion fairly much along the lines of their teacher's own intellectual process. The faithful began to rely more and more upon formal instruction, often in a tutorial or classroom environment. Religious instruction became more complex with each generation, as the theological concepts began to evolve.

After the Reformation spirituality went through one of its periodic confusions with emotional excesses. There was a sentimental and romantic pietism which would at times erupt into quite bizarre behavior. Many Christians reacted against these emotional outbursts and felt more comfortable in abstract theological expressions of faith. One of the most interesting attempts at balance was the increased use of hymn singing, which developed first in Protestant congregations and steadily became more universal. The music and the associated devotionalism would tend to be left-handed, whereas the actual text was often right-handed, thereby creating a popular equilibrium.

By and large, however, there continued to be an atrophication of the left hand in Christian formation. This had a negative effect upon life in general because spiritual growth was one of the traditional ways in which we developed the right hemisphere (left hand), and increased tendencies toward the symbolic and poetic in the average person. Without exercise these intuitive functions begin to decrease. Today we have greatly extended our left hemispheric (right hand) activities through the computer. The corresponding deficiency of the right hemisphere (left hand) affects not only the spiritual aspect of existence, but life itself.

Thesis: Formal Religious Education

By the twentieth century most parents felt inadequate to handle the Christian education of their children. However, formal religious subject matter taught in out-of-home classroom settings has been universally criticized in this century. It should be remembered that our contemporary experience is only a small part of the entire history of Christian education. In effect, what we may be doing at this time is questioning the continuation of the present model. In the latter part of the century we are in a delicate transition period.

Independent of any religious considerations, this has also been a rapidly changing period in American history. In fact our major psychological and social problem today may be our ability to adapt interiorly to rapid change.

In the final decades of the twentieth century the general tendency is not so much to find social solutions to our common problems as to discover individual ways of slowing down the rate of change There is increasing voluntary non-participation in such matters as electronic entertainment. Movements to return to the land have become common. There are redefinitions of professional success and attempts to humanize important aspects of life. These private escapes are important and deserve affirmation. Nonetheless, they do create an even greater distance between the various elements of our society, thereby helping to shatter the already fragile fabric of community. In the United States we are a very "successful" people, many of whom have longings that will never be fulfilled.

In this changing period religion will often be identified with the past. A recent study found that over fifty percent of the Roman Catholic dropouts under the age of twenty-two did so because of an identification of religion with the "old ways" of their parents. Their rebellion was more of a generational problem than a spiritual one. The young people had never internalized or identified personally with the Catholic Church. In other words, the relevance of religion in the life of the parent has not been translated to the world of the child. Young adults know that their world is certainly different from their parents' world, and religion is simply a part of that difference.[3]

Parochial school, the weekly religion class, and the Sunday school are presently seen by most parents, children, teachers and pastors alike as the primary place for Christian education.

This phenomenon was intentionally furthered by the Catholic Church in this country because of the minority mentality and the great fear of being absorbed into the surrounding Protestant culture. Reservations were expressed about the abilty of immigrant parents to handle the problem. In 1915 Archbishop John Ireland wrote:

> The place to teach religion is the school-room. . . . As a matter of fact, religion is not taught in the home. Few parents are capable of teaching religion.

There was pressure on the teacher to use the limited time with the children in attempting to cram basic thinking into their heads. Until recently no tool was believed to be as effective in assisting the teacher as had been the Baltimore Catechism of the late nineteenth century. The catechism was to help children respond to questions they would encounter in an alien Protestant environment during their adult life. It simply required memorization of codes and concepts.

In American Protestant religious education and in British lower schools the emphasis was more upon biblical knowledge rather than catechism. The child had great difficulty understanding the theological concepts. Ronald Goldman, a British educational psychologist, made an important study of the actual results of this type of education. He discovered that the biblical principle that "man does not live by bread alone" normally conveys to a young child only a question as to whether the bread is to be supplemented by honey, butter or jam.[4] Along a similar line, I vividly remember witnessing a first grade class being taught the creation story. Afterward, I talked for some time to a child who was fascinated by the fact that God was a truck driver. The teacher had made the point that "God drove Adam and Eve out of the garden." The child was quite happy that he finally knew what people were talking about when they used the word "God." But one could foresee future problems, not only in this youngster's religious experience but in his approach to truck drivers.

Antithesis: Faith Development

Neither the Catholic catechism nor the Protestant biblical study was appropriate for young children. We can say that these two models were the thesis of Christian education in the first part of the twentieth century. A major change occurred in the middle of the century, partly under the generally freeing influence of Vatican II. Religious educators began to look for support among developmental psychologists, such as Jean Piaget, and neo-Freudians, like Erik Erikson. Educators increasingly questioned the primary emphasis upon childhood to the exclusion of the other stages of life. They called for a concept of "faith development" in which the appropriate questions were raised at the proper chronological age. In fact, this approach went so far in some quarters as to begin to seriously question the appropriateness of attempting to educate the young child at all.

We have an ironic situation in which we encouraged Christian education to be taken from the home, found that it was not an appropriate subject matter for the classroom, and, instead of returning it to the home, simply continued anyway or effectively abandoned the whole process.

I am not unsympathetic to the frustrations of long-term Christian educators, watching generation after generation of fairly non-productive work in this century. A Church leader wrote to me:

> I have real wonderings about "good" religious education with children. Later, when they rebel, they rebel against something good instead of something bad in religion. Then, when and if they come back, they must accept something they once rejected. If they had bad religious education they can just forget it and rejoice in the new discovery without having to accept that which they had once rejected.

Although it is not often expressed so openly, there certainly is evidence of a decreasing interest in the Christian education of young children. Much of what was taught in the classroom was not significant, or retained. The emphasis has more and more been placed on those ages in which young people could understand the same concepts that were exciting to their teachers. There was, in other words, a new world beginning to open in religion, and the teachers wanted to address themselves to those students who would be able to understand it.

This situation became the antithesis in our twentieth century historical development of religious education.

The Community Synthesis

Now we are at the beginning of a synthesis, which is an attempt to modify both the thesis and the antithesis. We can term this the *community* approach, borrowing from John Westerhoff's concept that "the context or place of religious education needs to be changed from an emphasis on schooling to a community of faith."[5] One of the aspects of this approach is the realization by leaders like Westerhoff and Goldman that, whereas the attempt to cram abstract thoughts into children's heads is inappropriate, there are other aspects of Christian education which should be introduced in childhood. Piaget and other developmental psychologists were relevant only for the aspects of religious education (right hand) and have little to say about spiritual growth (left hand).

Unconditional reliance upon the "faith development" antithesis can lead us to difficulties reminiscent of our problems with progressive education. I have attempted to draw this parallel in more detail in Appendix B. For our purposes here perhaps it is enough to share the observation of educational psychologist Bob Samples:

> The reason for challenging the rational, linear, culturally ordered constructs that now define the human mind is that in reality they are a half-minded portrait at best. *Piaget's constructs describe only the function of the left cerebral (right hand) hemisphere in most humans!*[6]

The evolving community synthesis can be used in the early years of life for facilitating predominantly the left-handed aspects of Christian education. This will require that we seriously proceed to develop a program of spiritual formation that will lay the foundation for later religious education. The best environment for this formation is in the home, but we are in a transition period and parents will need considerable assistance.

A Child's Natural Interest

One more observation is relevant to the need for a synthesis in our approach to formation. Children are naturally spiritually inquisitive. They will not wait for a nicely organized high school age religious education program to begin their explorations. There is no question about young children receiving spiritual education, even if they live in a militant anti-religious environment. The only issue is: Will their spiritual education be confused and distorted or will it be a constructive grafting to their cultural roots which will be of assistance in preparing them for their later life?

A secondary observation relates to the phenomenon of young people from "good Catholic," "good Methodist" and "good" anything else homes who are flocking to every variety of Eastern and Near Eastern spirituality. These are almost always left-handed spiritual experiences. The issue is: Will we help our children discover this kind of experience in early life, or will we later simply help them look up the nearest Zen roshi to whom we will turn over our obligations as the spiritual guides of our children?

Stages of Growth

Until comparatively recently we did not believe that children were anything more than "little adults." The medieval attitude was simple:

> The first stage is childhood when the teeth are planted, and this age begins when the child is born and lasts until seven, and in this age that which is born is called an infant, which is as good as saying not talking, because in this age it cannot talk well or form its words perfectly, for its teeth are not yet well arranged or firmly implanted. . . . After infancy comes

the second age. . . . It is called *pueritia* and is given this name because in this age the person is still like the pupil in the eye, as Isidora says, and this age lasts till fourteen.[7]

Children were generally not even portrayed in medieval art before approximately the twelfth century. Prior to that time if it was necessary for children to be depicted in the myth or scriptural story being illustrated they were usually painted as small adults. There were no special clothes for children as late as the thirteenth century. Youngsters simply went from their swaddling clothes to small adult dress. Many of our present attitudes toward spiritual growth and religious development had their roots in the medieval period which was obviously influenced by the prevailing attitude toward early childhood.

In the 1970's, as was mentioned above, we saw the rise of "faith development" which attacked the premise that children are miniature adults. The first approaches were indebted to the work of developmental psychologists Jean Piaget and later Lawrence Kohlberg, focusing on the child's capacity for resolving moral conflicts. This was specifically applied to religious education by James Fowler.

Gradually, the faith development concept expanded to more internalized processes, and the work of the neo-Freudian psychoanalyst Erik Erikson has been extremely influential among religious educators. Erikson outlines eight ages of humans.[8] The following is a listing of (1) the age and (2) Erikson's concept of the basic issues to be resolved in the chronological period. In parentheses are what he calls the "basic virtue" characteristic of each period. He sees these basic virtues as being built into the blueprint of human development through our process of cultural evolution, and therefore we can rely upon them to re-emerge from generation to generation.

Early Infancy: Basic trust vs. basic mistrust (hope)
Later Infancy: Autonomy vs. shame and doubt (will-power)
Early Childhood: Initiative vs. guilt (purpose)
Later Childhood: Industry vs. inferiority (competency)
Adolescence: Identity vs. role confusion (fidelity)
Young Adulthood: Intimacy vs. isolation (love)

Older Adulthood: Generativity vs. stagnation (care)
Full Maturity: Ego integrity vs. despair (wisdom)

As freeing as these developmental psychoanalytic concepts have proven to be to some educators, they do not present the entire picture of a child's growth.

The National Catechetical Directory (NCD) for Roman Catholics of the United States, published by the National Conference of Catholic Bishops in November 1977, and approved by the Vatican the following year,[9] follows rather closely the concepts of Erikson but adapts them to the development of faith as applied to formation in the pre-adolescent period. The NCD recommendations for young children have, as yet, not been satisfactorily implemented. The following concrete suggestions and objectives are put forward in the NCD.

For the period of early *infancy* those who come in contact with children are urged to "speak naturally and simply about God and their faith." The suggestion is that the child be encourage to pray by "parental example." Programs for pre-school children should be designed to assist children to "seek to foster their growth in a wider faith community."[10] In the *early childhood* period (ages 3–5) appropriate attitudes of worship are encouraged by "occasions of natural celebration." We are urged to deepen the child's "sense of wonder and awe, to develop the capacity for spontaneous prayer and prayerful silence." It is further suggested that the learning process be "fostered through coordinated courses for the entire family, which help parents become active, confident and competent in encouraging their children's emerging faith."

The NCD recommends *childhood* (ages 6–10) programs which seek to call the child's attention "to God's self-revelation and his invitation to us to be his children and friends." The immediate environment for this type of development is the home, but it is recognized that there must be a cooperative relationship between the home and the larger community, which will absorb the school experience. The catechist is also urged to help children make an "increasingly personal response to God's word and gifts."

The *pre-adolescent period* (ages 10–13) must somehow

take into account the beginning "rapid, radical change" that the child is experiencing, and the example of "living faith" that he or she finds at home and in the larger community remains of tremendous influence.

The suggestions in this book are basically consistent with the NCD, which recognizes that faith calls for a solid spiritual, as well as religious, response.

No Single Psychological School

The NCD contains an important warning that no particular behavioral science approach should be used exclusively.[11] This is a wise caution. The various psychological schools are good for different purposes, but it is the responsibility of the Christian educator to harvest the best from all of them. Certainly the developmental theories were useful in questioning the ineffective and counter-productive models of early twentieth century religious education. The neo-Freudian psychoanalytical approach taught us much about the process of internalizing the moral (right and wrong) decisions. However, when we approach spiritual growth it is well to consider a broader psychological spectrum. This will be presented in the next chapter.

5. Humanistic Psychology and Spiritual Growth

When the time comes to design specific spiritual programs for young people, many parents and educators turn to existential approaches to psychology. They look for models which emphasize the value and uniqueness of each individual with resulting concerns for freedom and authenticity. This phenomenon usually goes under the broad category of "humanistic psychology."

Psychological Types

The psychology of Carl Jung has great popularity today. Jung is concerned with a person's deep inner experiences. Many have been introduced to these experiences by such practical professionals as Ira Progoff with his journal-keeping methods. Depth psychology has been admirably absorbed into Christian education through the tireless efforts of Morton Kelsey.

Perhaps the most practical Jungian contribution to the spiritual formation of children is to be found in his work on psychological types. Sixteen basic human types are suggested, each with its own characteristic way of perceiving and organizing information. It has been suggested by Kelsey that the failure to recognize these differing types has been a fundamental reason for Christianity's painful divisions over prayer, ritual and religious life-styles. Jung himself suggested that the failure to realize these fundamental human preferences is the reason for the great theological divisions of the Middle Ages between those emphasizing reason [right hand?] and those emphasizing revelation [left hand?].¹

The best practical exploration of Jungian typology is found in the work of Isabel Briggs-Meyers. Her work has been made available to large numbers of people in recent years through the easily administered "Briggs-Meyers Type Indicator" test, now in regular use at many retreat centers and schools. As a result many parents and teachers are now able to better understand that in any group of children there are radically different interior processes. Even when these youngsters are supposedly facing the same issue they can be expected to comprehend and absorb information, and to act on it, in quite different ways.

Briggs-Meyers suggests a relationship between early childhood training and the subsequent development of psychological preference. She sees two basic spirals for children. The upward spiral, leading to maturity, is characterized by the child being willing to make an effort "aimed beyond the impulse of the moment." The downward spiral basically results in children doing what they please. "Undeveloped people would rather do as they please than make such an effort, and all children are undeveloped to begin with. . . . What children need is the conviction that *satisfaction can and must be earned.*"² Spoiled children learn to blame everything on an outside cause. At the other end of the scale, extremely discouraged or "under-indulged" children never learn that satisfaction can be earned. As either spoiled or discouraged children age, they, in effect, choose not to mature psychologically and instead remain on a childish level. Such a situation as Briggs-Meyers describes can have a profound effect upon an individual's capacity for spiritual development. For example, spoiled or discouraged children can well grow into men or women who will only engage in religious or spiritual activity if it "makes" them feel happy. They can rarely be motivated to persevere toward a deeper satisfaction should it require any amount of uncomfortable confrontation with personal values or attitudes. This is an especially serious problem today in affluent churches. Retreats of youth groups from wealthy areas often reveal young people's inability to comprehend a life-style that would require them to do anything against their will. As Briggs-Meyers says, "Spoiled children do not learn the *must.*"[3] These youngsters will not consider a delayed satisfaction such as the experience of solitude or prayer. Equally, they will not consider seeing, for example, the poor of the world as in any real sense connected with them. The child's involvement with social issues is dependent upon how much immediate satisfaction he or she might receive from helping an unfortunate.

The foregoing observation raises a serious question about the popular "laid back" attitude that children ought to be continually emotionally satisfied in order to be reached. According to Briggs-Meyers, to cooperate in this process will almost surely guarantee that "physical maturity arrives without psychological maturity."[4]

The Development of Personality

Having explored individual psychological types and recgonized that they exist, let us attempt to get an operational sense of a child's basic nature. This is usually referred to as personality theory, by which we attempt to increase our understanding of a particular child's behavior.

This inquiry is important for spiritual formation, which must take place within the context of each child's general personality development. In other words, a child will have an overall agenda for life at any given time, and his or her concerns in that regard may well overshadow the spiritual dimension. Religious and spiritual facts become like any other facts, and are absorbed and utilized in accordance with the developing personality.

In the past decade a considerable number of parents and teachers have found great practical assistance in the works of the late psychiatrist Rudolf Dreikurs. Dreikurs' many works on children, marriage and education are practical applications of the work of his teacher, Alfred Adler, the founder of the school of individual psychology. Dreikurs freely admits that his personality theory, which is based on wholistic philosophy, is subjective. But he suggests that this is true of all personality theory. His approach worked well and is based on years of extensive professional experience as a psychiatrist and educator. The major points of Dreikurs' theory can be set forth briefly:[5]

1. *All behavior has social meaning.* This is in contrast to theories which hold that a child's behavior is the result either of heredity (some Freudians) or environment (behaviorists). Social striving is seen as primary. The child must never be viewed in isolation but in relation to other human beings. Conflicts are the result of interpersonal situations, not intrapersonal difficulties.

2. *All behavior is purposive.* This challenges the view that behavior is "caused" by any particular set of circumstances. Instead we are urged to look for goals that will explain actions. Only the consequences of behavior are capable of being observed, and any statement about possible causes is speculative.

3. *The child must be viewed subjectively.* We are not influenced by facts as such, but rather by our particular interpretation and reaction to these facts. It is more important to know how a child feels than to know the concrete details of a particular act. All behavior makes sense to the child in terms of his or her own *private logic.* The significance of a past experience depends on the way in which an individual child has come to interpret that experience.

4. *The child has the creative power to make personalized decisions.* This is in opposition to a stimulus-response theory of behavior. In other words, the child is not simply a receiver of external stimuli. Children have the creative power to interpret and assign individual meaning to all that goes on around them. There is a tendency for children to perceive only what they want to see. A person's uniqueness relates to what that individual perceives and how he or she reacts to that perception. Thus, one person can see what another cannot, and children who perceive the same circumstance can react to it quite differently. The child, then, is not at the mercy of particular drives, nor the victim of impulses, nor are his or her actions determined by environment, heredity, or organic forces. Rather the child is able to exercise a considerable freedom of choice in any circumstance.

5. *Belonging is the child's basic need.* Children want to belong to something or someone in a special way. This is usually

worked out in the *family constellation* where a particular child occupies a unique position, one which no one else in the family occupies. This dynamic leads to the development of the child's individual life-style or basic operational approach to living. Difficulties in the area of belonging lead to fear, anxiety, and psychological distortion. For example, I can grow up believing that I can belong, that is, have a place, only "if I am in control," or "only if I am intellectually superior," or "only if I find a strong person to take care of me."

On the other hand early training can lead to an attitude of security and cooperation which will result in the development of a sense of *social interest,* that is, a concern for the common welfare. Adler invented this term, which is *gemeinschafts gefuhl* in German. Today we might describe this as a feeling of solidarity with the human community.

6. *The approach to children's behavior and training must be wholistic.* This opposes an attempt to reduce an individual to the sum total of any particular set of attitudes or processes which may be found in a person's makeup. "You can tear a mosaic down to its individual pieces," Dreikurs once lectured me. "You can count them, sort them according to color, size and weight, and do anything else you want to with them, but when you are finished, all you will be able to discuss is pieces! You are no longer able to describe the mosaic." A child is a unified psycho-biological-spiritual organism. It is simply not possible or necessary to accurately analyze that child's behavior, since children reveal themselves through their movements and relations with the world around them.

In Briggs-Meyers and Dreikurs we have explored applications of alternatives to Freud developed in Europe by Alfred Adler and Carl Jung. Let us turn to a uniquely American approach.

Self-Actualization

Abraham Maslow was an optimistic psychologist who helped turn psychology away from preoccupation with abnormal concerns. Although proceeding from an agnostic position theologically, he had an early and continuing interest in spiritual matters which has endeared him to the American religious community. Despite frequent physical problems he had an infectious positive attitude that impressed even his critics.

Maslow's study of psychological health brought him continually into the spiritual field. In 1963, in lectures later published as *Religions, Values and Peak Experiences,* [6] he criticized the overly intellectual rationalism of so-called "liberal" religions which attempted to rely primarily on natural science:

> The result? A rather bleak, boring, unexciting, unemotional, cool philosophy of life which fails to do what the traditional religions have tried to do when they were at their best, to inspire, to awe, to comfort, to fulfill, to guide in the value choices, and to discriminate between higher and lower, better and worse, not to mention to produce Dionysiac experiences, wildness, rejoicing, impulsiveness. [7]

And he accurately predicted a dwindling influence of these intellectualized religious groups because

> . . . they base themselves upon a lopsided picture of human nature which omits most of what human beings value, enjoy, and cherish in themselves, in fact, which they live for, and which they refuse to be done out of. [8]

Spirituality was a subdivision of Maslow's general interest in the psychology of health, or, as he was fond of saying, "of the human being at his best." The term which became associated with Maslow was the "self-actualizing person," that is, an individual fully using and exploiting his or her talents, capacities and potentials. Among the many characteristics that he observed in self-actualizing people are a number which are of particular importance to Christian educators. What follows is not a complete catalogue of Maslow's observations but just a few relating to our present concerns.

Maslow found that behavior in self-actualizing individuals was marked with simplicity, naturalness and a lack of artificiality. There was no straining for effect but rather a refreshing spontaneity. The individuals were not fascinated by or focused exclusively on themselves. They could attack problems outside

of themselves with no references to what personal consequences might result. There was also the quality of detachment
from being emotionally involved with petty annoyances. In most
cases there was a positive desire for solitude and privacy. There
was also a special quality:

> Self-actualizing people have the wonderful capacity to ap-
> preciate again and again, freshly and naively, the basic
> goods of life, with awe, pleasure, wonder, and even ecstasy,
> however stale these experiences may have become to oth-
> ers.[9]

Maslow also discovered Adler's "social interest" in self-actualizing people as well as a deep capacity for love, coupled
with a delightful appetite for thoroughly enjoying themselves
without apology. There was an absence of authority rebellion.
Present also was a good sense of right and wrong, without much
hesitation. There was a freedom from the limitations of the age
in which they lived and a resulting creativeness.

Perhaps for our purposes the most significant observation
was the recurrence in self-actualizing people of what Maslow
terms the "peak experience." This is not an entirely satisfactory
term. Many urged him to adopt either a more creative term or
the traditional spiritual vocabulary. In his later life Maslow
sometimes coupled "peak" and "mystic," but he did not want
to see the process shrouded in a pseudo-religious somberness.
Nonetheless, the phenomenon itself, which he found had been
experienced by his subjects, is one common to Christian spirituality. It is a proposition of this book that the "peak experience"
must be a part of childhood if Christian formation is to have a
lasting effect upon the adult life of the child.

How can this "peak experience" be described?

> . . . feelings of limitless horizons opening up to the vision,
> the feeling of being simultaneously more powerful and also
> more helpless than one ever was before, the feeling of great
> ecstasy and wonder and awe, the loss of placing in time and
> space with, finally, the conviction that something extremely
> important and valuable had happened, so that the subject is
> to some extent transformed and strengthened even in his
> daily life by such experiences.[10]

Does this seem too much to expect to happen to children we know? For a quarter of a century I have encouraged adults to reflect upon their personal spiritual history and to recall details from their memories of early childhood. Over and over I have listened to experiences that would fit Maslow's description. I am convinced that it is a natural part of childhood. The Christian educator must help to arrange for the empty space necessary for this kind of experience to develop. A child who lacks this experience will be left with a shallow and easily discarded concept of spirituality.

Here we see such an important spiritual goal being put forward, not by a pietistic and cloistered romantic of past centuries, but by a non-theistic scientist of our own age.

But are there any practical guidelines on how we can educate for "peak experiences"? Maslow has suggested that anyone who believes that he can make children into anything has never had a child. One of the points I believe he would emphasize today in the present climate is for the Christian educator to really believe that "the human being *has higher needs,* that he has instinct-like needs, which are a part of his biological equipment."[11] I would interpret this to mean that we approach the spiritual with more confidence.

The lesson we can learn from Maslow is that the "peak experience" is not an unusual supernatural phenomenon, but is naturally experienced by practically everyone in some way or another. What is lacking is a social framework that helps absorb the experience into our life-style and our comprehension of reality.

In other words, Maslow, inadvertently, is urging us as Christian educators to really believe in the spiritual dimension and to convey this belief to the young people who look to us for guidance.

Social Patterns
Humanistic psychology helps us to appreciate the individual nature of the interior development of each child. While remembering this unique psychological nature, we can, nonetheless, with safety, attempt to get a general overview of

the religious and spiritual process in children. It is important, however, that these operational guidelines be used with the understanding that there are many individual exceptions.

The best experts are probably grandparents who have been involved with a large number of children covering several generations. Failing that, we turn to humanistically inclined social psychologists. Gordon Allport stands out as one of the most significant contributors in this field.[12] Allport maintains a helpful distinction between those individuals who do or do not approach religion for what it can do for them. This attitude may be conscious or unconscious. For those who do have an *extrinsic* interest the issue is: Can their religious activity produce a better marriage, more professional clients or customers, rewards in the afterlife or less trouble from their kids? The religious interest of these people is basically self-centered. On the other hand are those who approach religion in a more *intrinsic* fashion.

Let us explore Allport's attitude toward "the religion of youth."[13] In general the religion of youngsters is quite egocentric, and this attitude is in many cases likely to continue into adult life. Allport maintains that the religion of the young child is quite different from the religion of the adult. He feels that in infancy religion is lacking. This is a position which I can appreciate, but it is nonetheless one with which I disagree.

The first religious activities for the young child are not, Allport insists, religious at all, but entirely social, and such little habits as bowing the head, folding the hands, and reciting prayers and hymns have nothing to do with the child's relationship to the divine but rather to his or her parents.

It is important to remember that Allport's major point— namely, the child's world is very self-centered and that he cannot "separate thought and feeling from the reality of the external world; by thinking things he makes them happen"—is quite true. We may be impressed as little Johnny says his prayers or looks particularly holy in church. In fact, however, what is going on inside of little Johnny can be a trifle terrifying. Allport supports Piaget's[14] proposition that the young child can even go so far as to believe that the sun exists for no other reason than to follow him wherever he goes. Natural phenomena, like thunderstorms, are thought to be special punishments. Santa Claus, often equated with God, has no interest except watching the particular child.

Of especial importance to Christian educators, especially parents, is Allport's following proposition:

> What is taught turns out in the long run to be less important than the manner of teaching. Quite apart from the content of his lessons, the child gains an indelible impression of the sincerity of his parents. Their tone of voice, their example in daily living, are not lost on the child, even though it may be years before he fully recognizes or appreciates their deep-lying piety.[15]

In attempting to comprehend the almost universal religious crises of high school and college age students, I have gained appreciation for Allport's position. Even though a child may rebel against parents' belief systems or practices, often a deep underlying spiritual sentiment has been conveyed from parent to child, which in times of difficulty will come forth as a support system. This underscores again the need to take seriously the religious and spiritual development of the young child. We cannot simply settle some of the basics and then wait until he or she is old enough to "intelligently" comprehend the stepping stones of faith. Unless we instill a spiritual sentiment early, there probably is not going to be any later stage in the child's development. The crisis in faith seems to be developing at an earlier and earlier age among our youth.

Although disagreeing with Freud that people inevitably confuse God with their physical father, Allport does indicate that the child approaches the spiritual in an anthropomorphic way, and is looking toward some kind of God in the sky, who is almost always a male. When the child's self-centered prayers are not answered, or when there is some tragedy, such as the death of a puppy or a gift not arriving for Christmas, there is a tendency for the child to begin the process of abandoning religion as an unproductive method for obtaining desires.

Another phenomenon which Allport observes goes slightly beyond our concerns, but its roots are laid in this early childhood period. Two-thirds of all children have a reaction against parental and cultural teaching, and half of those rebellions come before the age of sixteen and half later, with girls entering the period sooner than boys. But Allport also points out that the average age for deep conversion is at about the same time, and seems to be getting younger. In other words, fundamental options in life are coming critically near the end of the period in which the child is dependent upon his family for a sense of the world.

6. Eastern Insights

Before leaving this section on the growth process, let us take a look at two examples from outside of our own culture.

Hindu

In Asian spirituality the necessity for early formation has long been accepted. In Hindu India this spiritual progress is evidenced by an evolution of four life vocations: student, householder, contemplative, and sage. The counsel that a person who has raised a family and is engaging in a career should change life-styles at a certain point and become a contemplative is alien to our traditional sense of lifelong vocations. But new attitudes are emerging in the West and second careers or vocations are becoming more common. The Indian process is an all-consuming one, as Rabindranath Tagore explained:

> As the day is divided into morning, noon, afternoon and evening, so India has divided man's life into four parts, following the requirements of his nature. The day has the waxing and waning of its light; so has man the waxing and waning of his bodily powers. Acknowledging this, India gave a connected meaning to his life from start to finish.
>
> First came *brahmacharya,* the period of discipline and education; then *garhasthya,* that of the world's work; then *vanaprasthya,* the retreat for the loosening of bonds; and finally, *pravrajya,* the expectant awaiting of freedom across death.[1]

The process is to move from the individual to the community, from the community to the universal, and from the universal to infinity.

For the purposes of the concerns in this book it should be emphasized that all of these stages depend upon the first one: the training of the young child in what Tagore called the "period of discipline and education." The "householder" period usually began in what we think of today as adolescence. The earlier student period was taken most seriously according to Tagore:

> Our teachers, therefore, keeping in mind the goal of this progress, did not, in life's first stage of education, prescribe merely the learning of books or things, but *brahmacharya,* the living in discipline, whereby both enjoyment and its renunciation would come with equal ease to the strengthened character.[2]

I find a strong comparison between the Asian spiritual teacher and the American athletic coach. If we undertook spiritual training with all of the vigor and discipline we use in athletics, our children would be much better off than they are at present.

The first stage (student) and the third stage (contemplative) of life are seen as a kind of completed circle or spiral. The central issue in both cases is training. The person, whether child or elder, requires appropriate training in order to adapt and utilize the new freedom now coming into his or her life. This training is a matter of great importance and of urgency—attitudes often lacking in our own approach to Christian education.

Tibetan Buddhism

Buddhism, at least as it developed in Tibet, integrated naturally with psychology. This was the case with Christianity well into the Middle Ages,[3] but it certainly has not been true in recent centuries, until the last decade. Contemporary researchers present a more unified approach in some parts of the East where the psychological development of a person is central to the religious experience.[4]

The five traditional stages of growth in Tibetan Buddhism are:

1. *Tshogs-lam.* This is the *preparatory* way, the stage of accumulating what is necessary for a person's intellectual and spiritual growth. This will be discussed in more detail below.

2. *Sdyor-lam.* This is the way of *aspiration.* It is a link between what has been learned and future growth. In this stage the desire for the spiritual quest has awakened. The connection between everyday life and that eventual enlightenment has been realized.

3. *Nthong-lam.* This is the way of *seeing.* A person begins to grasp the intrinsic nature, not only of the self but also of the universe. Here he or she recognizes such things as the four noble truths (suffering does in fact exist, it is the result of certain causes, the cessation of suffering is possible, and there is a path which would end suffering). This attitude is developed in a growing awareness of community and compassion.

4. *Sgom-lam.* This is the way of intensive spiritual *practice.* It leads to a living experience of the spiritual way with a deep awakening and an increased awareness.

5. *Mi-slob-lam.* This is the way of *Buddhahood.* We are fulfilled in enlightenment and become one with the basic harmony and unity of life. We enter the "Omega point," to borrow a phrase from Teilhard de Chardin.

Let us return to the first stage, the *preparatory* way. This path is not simply a waiting time until the child can develop enough sensitivity to perceive true spirituality. Quite the contrary, it is an essential foundation for the other steps.

One of the most striking characteristics of *tshogs-lam* is the integration of the cognitive and the non-cognitive processes. The undeserved reputation of Buddhism in this country as being anti-intellectual comes from the fact that most American Buddhists enter after childhood. In these cases Buddhism is being grafted onto the experiences of an American childhood, which most often have had a rather one-sided emphasis on the cognitive. Buddhism in America is then seen as an antidote to overly-formalized thought systems and practices. But to a Tibetan Buddhist child no such antidote would be necessary. The spiritual dimension is seen as a post-intellectual assistance in the assimilation of various life experiences. At no time does a Tibetan Buddhist child expect that intellectual or rational pursuits will provide him or her with spiritual fulfillment, any more than mathematics would be expected to develop our leg muscles. Consequently, the confusions, conflicts, and frustrations of late adolescence so characteristic in the West are supposedly largely avoided through Buddhistic formation. Buddhist psychologists warn that troubled adults are often found to have fixated at an immature level in the childhood development pattern. Without the spiritual dimension we can be in serious difficulty.

> As life-experiences accumulate, we are lost in a fragmented
> and narrow world of socially defined roles, opinions, biases,
> speculations, and bits and pieces of knowledge.[5]

An actual glimpse of the process of formation in childhood is supplied by Chogyam Trungpa. Trungpa has made the incredible leap from being an incarnate high-ranking lama and supreme abbot of a large monastic complex in Tibet to becoming a Westernized spiritual teacher who has considerable current popularity with American young people. He was found and accepted as the lama when he was very young. At the age of five he was put in charge of the monks he was later to rule as abbot. The following excerpts are taken from his book, *Born in Tibet:*[6]

> My own time-table was as follows: I rose with my tutor at
> five for the first morning devotions, then we were given
> breakfast, after which my reading lesson went on until mid-
> day; this was followed by a meal and half an hour's rest.
> Then I was given a writing lesson for half an hour and again
> reading until the evening. . . . On special afternoons we
> went for walks and then, in the evening, we practiced chant-

ing. I loved going out with Asang Lama [his tutor]; he used to tell me stories about the life of the Buddha and at other times about the Tenth Trungpa Tulku [Chogyam Trungpa was the Eleventh Trungpa Tulku]. I was fascinated also to find so many wild flowers on the hills as well as sweet scented juniper bushes. There were all sorts of birds and animals, and the blackbirds especially were so tame that their songs could be heard all around the centre and they would come for food to the window sills.[7]

The love and respect of Trungpa's tutor and his sense of responsibility for the future life of this child is humorously but poignantly developed in this excerpt:

When he thought that it was necessary to admonish me, it was always done with great ceremony. After a foreword, such as, "It is like moulding an image; it has to be hammered into shape," he would prostrate himself three times before me and then administer the chastisement on the appropriate part.[8]

When Trungpa was eight years old he learned to perform the various rites and to use the drums and bells and other instruments associated with religious ceremony. He was also introduced to the practice and history of Buddhism, but not on an exclusively intellectual level.

When I read about the death of his [the Buddha's] mother seven days after his birth, I seemed to share his feeling of loss.[9]

In the Tibetan Buddhist approach no attempt was made to rely exclusively on short periods of religious instruction:

At eight years old a child is very sensitive, and it is the time to inculcate ideas which must last him his lifetime, so at the end of this year I went into a retreat for a simple form of meditation. This was upon the *nyendrup* of Manjusri, the Bodhisattva of Wisdom: that is to say, I was instructed to visualize him with his various symbolic attributes, and to contemplate his transcendental Wisdom, to repeat his *mantras* or sonorous embodiments, and to recite the verses which preceded and followed them. I took a vow that I would live in solitude for three months away from all contacts other than my tutor and my cook attendant; no one might come to see me. My diet was strictly vegetarian, and I was not allowed to go outside the retreat centre. This continued until the New Year.[10]

There had been two primary religious teachers in Trungpa's life. The third and last major teacher of his childhood came when he was nine years old.

When I first saw him, I was enormously impressed; he was so different from any other teacher that I had met. He was a big jolly man, friendly to all without distinction of rank, very generous and with a great sense of humor combined with deep understanding; he was always sympathetic to the troubles of others. Though he was not well at the time, to be near him was to experience unbelievable peace and joyfulness. He used to say that now that we had met again he was my teacher as, the time before, my predecessor had been his. He so clearly remembered all that the tenth Trungpa Tulku had taught him, and all his kindness to him from his earliest childhood. He said how happy he was to give back to me that which he had received from his own *guru,* or as they say in Tibet, "to return the owner's possessions."[11]

Had the custom of returning "the owner's [God's] possessions" continued in Christianity we would not be floundering around as we are at present. In fact had we maintained the attitude of the apostolic age we would continue to fulfill our obligation to our children, our society and our faith by the single action of transmitting the good news to youngsters for whom we are responsible and there would be no need for this book. But we have walked another path.

Part III
THE SPIRITUAL
FORMATION
OF YOUNG
CHILDREN

7. The Guide

For the past quarter century I have been working with young people in a variety of different settings, in and out of the Church. I have related to them as a parent, godparent, guardian, teacher, counselor and spiritual director. One principle I have learned is that spiritual growth must take place on the child's home ground. Spiritual development must be an ongoing, twenty-four-hour, seven-day-a-week situation, which is as consistently a part of a youngster's upbringing as good grooming or nutrition. Religious education classes, brief encounters, retreats and even enrollment in a parochial school can all help, but the basic work must be in the home. This attitude is reflected in the NCD in referring to the pre-adolescent period.

> The immediate environment, normally the home, remains the principal setting in which the child experiences a relationship with God.[1]

The Parent as Guru

Parents are the natural and preferred spiritual directors of their children. At times in past ages this was considered a normal part of parenting. Instead of sending the children to groups, we should leave them at home and provide ongoing groups for the parents who might wish additional support.

This is not to say that programs which help develop a child's sense of religious community and literacy are not valuable. This would include all of the normal curriculum of religious education classes, especially that which traditionally centers around the sacramental milestones. In addition, youth retreats are certainly to be encouraged, provided they truly are spiritual and religious experiences led by people with a spiritual maturity. The fairly common complaints of parents about groups which turned out to be simply another "fun weekend" are unfortunately often justified.

Some of the most successful support programs in which I have participated have been mixed retreats, that is, where a parent and a child attend together. For example, a group of about a dozen pre-teen children of approximately the same age will each bring a parent to the retreat. The basic model calls for sessions in which the children gather around the leader while the parents sit back a way. For about twenty minutes a topic is explored between the children and the leader. Perhaps there may also be a meditation or reflection. For the balance of the hour the individual children go off alone with their parents to discuss, apply, or share reactions to what has been said. There are also some sessions just for the children and some just for the parents. In addition there are joint times of physical work and nature exploration. This program also helps break down little barriers which have blocked parents from being able to discuss spiritual topics with their children.

Foster Godparents

We have to face the reality that many parents are not prepared, for one reason or another, to take on the spiritual direction of their children. Technically, this responsibility would probably fall to the godparents, but this is usually not too practical and has not been taken seriously for centuries.

What is needed is a facilitator functioning between the fully involved parent and the teacher who sees a child for an hour each week. These intermediate persons can be seen as "foster godparents." What is being suggested is an understanding between parents, the child and the foster godparent that there will be an ongoing relationship by a particular person with a particular child as that child grows up. It is important that this be an explicit relationship with clear expectations of what is and is not appropriate. It is best to have this understanding verbalized quite near the beginning of the relationship. Whatever the specifics, it is the foster godparent's obligation to become involved in the child's spiritual growth process. This relationship should be formalized in some minimal way, perhaps through the actual use of the term "godmother" or "godfather," as labeling is often important in helping children understand a relationship. It would be well to have the foster godparent ministry affirmed by the local church through a special blessing or Communion.

In a large family the role of foster godparent often falls naturally upon a particular relative. Pope John XXIII's great-uncle Zaverio Roncalli, "Barba," was certainly an important spiritual mentor in the Pope's early life. "Barba" took his responsibilities seriously, and was appreciated by Pope John throughout his life. There is also Don Pedro DeCepeda, the uncle of Teresa of Avila, who was not above such crafty tricks as asking his young spiritually undisciplined niece to read aloud to him on one pretext or another, thus exposing her to concepts which he knew she would not explore on her own. Both of these foster godparents have earned the appreciation of all of us who have been influenced by the lives of these wonderful people.

Many teaching brothers and sisters have been informal foster godparents. Beginning with deep encounters in the classroom, they have followed a person's development into adult life. Such guides were often not at all shy about pointing out any suspected spiritual deficiency. Many of today's dedicated catechists are foster godparents, especially when there is geographical stability of both the family and the religious educator. Many more would be willing to take this step if they received the support and encouragement of the family and the local church community.

Prospective foster godparents will usually have an existing natural relationship to the child. Even so there will be a need to encourage people to consider seeing themselves in that light. Developing a foster godparent program would be a stimulating and creative ministry. Normally the ongoing support and training for foster godparents could be received in the parents' group suggested previously.

The Occasional Teacher

If there is neither a parent nor a foster godparent guiding the child, then the third option for a facilitator of spiritual growth is the religious educator who sees the child at most once a week and probably just for a few times before First Communion or confirmation. There is really not much that can be expected in the way of spiritual growth in such a short time. As a result we often focus exclusively on religious education. But when this is the only opportunity that might present itself, some emphasis should be put on spirituality as well as religious topics. In some ways a spark may often be kindled which will have significance in a child's later life. This will probably not result from the curriculum. The teacher's own spirituality can communicate something. Therefore, it is necessary to have teachers take seriously the need for their personal spiritual formation.

A child has a basic right to speak to a person who has prepared himself or herself on the major issues of Christian life. This is a fundamental issue which should never ever be compromised.

8. Spiritual Materialism

For those readers looking for concrete suggestions we have come to the heart of the book. Chapters 9 to 12 will outline a specific program with twelve steps. Before going to that program it is necessary to consider a basic pitfall.

One of the great lessons we can learn from Eastern spirituality is the danger of what the Buddhists have termed "gaining ideas." There are two basic approaches to spiritual growth. The first, and probably the more common, is to believe that we must pursue something new. We are reaching for something we do not have. We are attempting to "gain" something. This has also been referred to as "spiritual materialism." Even though there is a spiritual dimension to our quest, it is materialistic because of the amount of ego involved. "*I* will learn to meditate because *I* want more peace of mind."

The alternate approach is to assume that we are not to bring in something new, but that we are to become aware of something which we already have and have always had. This is a strong theme in Zen and Tibetan Buddhism. It is also present in the Tao Te Ching, as was noted previously in Chapter 3:

> In the pursuit of learning
>   every day something is added.
> In the pursuit of the Tao [the spiritual way]
>   every day something is dropped.[1]

Differing Teaching Theories

There is a basic distinction in pedagogical method between religious education and spiritual growth. No responsible reli-

gious educator is going to assume that a child can learn by os-
mosis. When a child is to be taught, for example, the lessons of
the Gospel, it obviously requires that there be an increase of
knowledge. Granted, there must be a certain amount of spiritual
reflection, but nonetheless there must be an increase of data.
Some new things are brought into the child's mental storehouse.
This is a quite different situation to teaching a child to pray,
which usually requires not the addition of anything, but the re-
moval of a great deal of emotional busyness.

The psalmist says, "Be still and know that I am God."[2] But
we are rarely still in our attempt to know God. Instead we are
worried about being bored or walking on an unproductive path.
We are fond of discovering new methods, gimmicks and tech-
niques. Such extraordinary states as ecstasy and trance, after
which some still strive, should be seen not as God's gift to his
elect but as his desperate way of crashing into our busy spiritual
world when all else had failed.[3]

America's Special Problem

Spiritual materialism is such an important factor in our
Western spiritual life, and especially in the United States, that it
cannot be overemphasized. A former Tibetan Buddhist abbot,
now living in this country, who has worked with many American young people, dramatically discerns our tendency to add
rather than to subtract in the spiritual life:

> But we have simply created a shop, an antique shop. We
> could be specializing in oriental antiques or medieval Chris-
> tian antiques or antiques from some other civilization or
> time, but we are, nonetheless, running a shop. Before we
> filled our shop with so many things the room was beautiful:
> white-washed walls and a very simple floor, with a bright
> lamp burning in the ceiling. There was an object of art in the
> middle of the room, and it was beautiful. Everyone who
> came appreciated its beauty, including ourselves.
>
> But we were not satisfied and we thought, "Since this one
> object makes my room so beautiful, if I get more antiques,

my room will be even more beautiful," so we began to collect, and the end result was chaos.

We searched the world over for beautiful objects—India, Japan, many different countries. And each time we found an antique, because we were dealing with only one object at a time, we saw it as beautiful and thought it would be beautiful in our shop. But when we brought the object home and put it there, it became just another addition to our junky collection. The beauty of the object did not radiate out any more, because it was surrounded by so many other beautiful things. It did not mean anything anymore. Instead of a room full of beautiful antiques we created a junk shop![4]

Some of us did not get into the spiritual junk business after having found a beautiful object in our own soul. Rather we have not turned the light on in that room and fear that there is not anything there.

It would be going too far to warn that "training exercises may be hazardous to your spiritual growth," but it is reasonable to convey a concern that we can easily fall in love with the signpost and forget to walk the road.

The Reactive Process

There must be a naturalness in the spiritual journey. Various teachers of Eastern and Western spirituality suggest that we attempt to be as we were "before we were born." It is difficult to comprehend the cosmic sense of this phrase, but on a practical level we are able to reflect on our life in the womb.

We are told that our early life was in several stages. The middle and end stages had moments of considerable anxiety, as we grew and our environment did not. But the first part of our life in the womb was quite another story. The egg grew much more rapidly than we, so that as we developed our world continually expanded. Our facial expressions were very relaxed and serene. All was quiet, warm and loving.

Then came the cramped period. We struggled and kicked, but eventually we submitted. We and our environment had a close relationship. In fact, physically we were one with the environment. All the sounds and perhaps the sights coming to us were muted and soft. Nothing was threatening.

In the final month before birth there was an especially joyful moment as the walls of our environment came alive with loving, playful caresses. It was a good time. We had experienced that sense of oneness we will in later life describe with such words as "centered," "wholeness," "unity with God."

Then came the great trial in which we were forced downward and crushed. We must have believed that we were being choked out of existence. But the inner strength from the past nine months helped us in the fight, which was probably the most heroic struggle of our entire existence. And so, with courage, in spite of the pain we went on to a point where it appeared that we had lost. Perhaps in the last few seconds we knew that death had come. But in fact we exploded into this noisy and busy world we would later come to call "life."

The critical point is that "before we were born" we adopted as our spiritual rhythm not a passive state nor an active state but a *reactive* stance. Often we believe in times of spiritual dryness that, for example in relation to prayer, if we do not "do something" nothing will "happen." In other words, we are so convinced that we must initiate the encounter with God that we frantically push forward. This is always counter-productive. Sometimes when we tire, or sense that our path has been too active, we go to the other extreme. We simply sit down and challenge God to handle the whole affair. Inevitably in either course we are disillusioned, and perhaps resentful.

Between these extremes is a reactive position in which we let God do his part and we do ours. It is much like a dance. We are not expected to provide the music and do the work of both partners. On the other hand we cannot simply sit on the sidelines. We assume that there will be music, if we listen. We accept that there will be a leading partner, if we are aware. To dance means that we simply react, follow the rhythm, and accept those times when it is right to be still. In those quiet times we have not disengaged, but in fact are very much connected with our partner and the song of life.

9. A Program for Spiritual Growth: Foundations

We now come to specific and pracitical suggestions. What follows is only one of many possible schemes. It is assumed that the twelve steps below are a point of departure for parents, foster godparents and teachers searching for an individual program for a particular child.

This program is taken from many sources, with a special indebtedness to spiritual formation concepts in Native American culture. Much that is here evolved from studies of Hopi and Sioux customs as well as experiencing the practices of some of the smaller Indian groups in California. There was great variation in the various Indian cultures, and many points that some would have considered important are not included here.

Preliminaries

This is a pre-adolescent program. It specifically urges that these twelve steps should be introduced from the first year of life on, and that all of them should be experienced before what William Blake termed the "age of innocence" has disappeared. Psychologically, adolescence is no longer equated to puberty. In some cases, even now, what is suggested here should be accomplished before the age of eight or nine.

Before beginning let us consider some underlying assumptions.

1. There are several chronological rhythms involved. There

should be a weekly, a monthly and a yearly "checklist." At each of these times go through these twelve points and see what each child has experienced in regard to each of them.

2. Bear in mind that you are not the only one working in this process. God is very much at work and needs an opportunity to communicate with the child. This means that the child is having a *personal experience* of God which can be disrupted by too much detailed inquiry or analysis on your part. The underlying attitude of the adult should be to do whatever will encourage the child to continue on the spiritual path.

3. It has been said that "silence is the language of heaven." Children, like adults, are sometimes nervous in the absence of conversation. An increased tolerance for *quiet* must be developed in the child. Silence is sometimes associated with discipline or punishment—being sent to a room, keeping still or standing in a corner. Therefore, positive aspects of quiet accompany all of the stages of this program. Whenever possible there should be an atmosphere of stillness.

The age for emphasis and even the sequence will change with different children. The reader's everyday life with a particular child will suggest opportunities to put the twelve steps into practice. Only by way of illustrating each step I have put down a few suggestions. These are set apart in italics.

Step 1. *Learning To Be at One with Nature*
The first step begins not with the unseen but with the seen. It is usually necessary to startle young children out of their self-occupation. This often means breaking a rhythm which a child is controlling. The natural process of learning normally corresponds with the child's desire to encounter the environment.

Stars
A simple example is to intentionally break the bedtime ritual, which tends to become formal very early. For example, if the child is usually put to bed by one parent, the other can come in one night. While encouraging an atmosphere of quiet, he or she can pick up the child (rather than giving a good-night kiss).

If it is a warm summer evening, carry the child outside, and while giving firm support, lift the child heavenward so that he or she can really see the stars and nothing else. This simple act can become a life ritual repeated at special times.

I have known this practice to be of considerable importance to older children too large to be easily held. A parent can stand behind them on a high point some evening and remind them of their place in this great and beautiful universe. Encouraging the attitude of silence, point the child's head upward. Leave your hands on the shoulders. In other words, give the feeling of both the warmness of home and the immensity of life.

There are many other simple and natural opportunities. These should never degenerate into a nature lesson. At all times these moments should be silent and, occasionally, even solemn. Physical contact is the key. Looking at a great ocean is not as significant for tiny children as being held in a backyard pool where they can experience the water covering their body without losing their sense of at-homeness. There should be many of these episodes in the early life of the child, but they should not be forgotten among the older children.

On the negative side, the child should be gently corrected for acts which evidence a separation from nature, for example, senseless destruction of life.

The Tree

When the child is a little older a good exercise is a carefully guided encounter with a large tree. If possible this tree should be one to which the child can return at times in his or her life. It is a good idea to repeat this exercise every year, especially at a family time, such as a birthday or camping trip. Begin by encouraging the child to fully experience the life of this tree. This is a being that does not walk around and yet has great strengths and a special place in creation. Encourage experiencing the tree as it really is. Guide the child to look at the tree very carefully and to see areas that might have been overlooked, such as the top crown, or right under the surface at the base. Look inside the bark: try to find scars and to under-

stand what happened. Feel the tree; try to embrace it. Have the child put his or her weight totally on the tree; become supported by it. Exercise all the other senses; feel with eyes closed; put an ear to the tree and listen to the creaking of the tree. Finally, after some time have the child sit down, lean against the tree and look up. With the back on the bark of the tree, get a sense of what it is like to be a tree. Contemplate the tree's history and its future. At this point the adult should simply go away for a while and let the child and the tree be alone. If the child experiences a feeling of wanting to talk to the tree (and many do) that is all right. This is not a time to be concerned about adult theological or psychological subtleties. Children talk to objects. It is part of their response to life.

Step 2. *Awareness of the Forces Around Us*

This is a natural extension of the first step. Again, we begin with nature. A child can be exposed to the violence of a windstorm by turning off the noisemakers in the house and asking the child to "be still and listen." If he or she has had the experience with the tree you might ask, "what do you think it is like for the tree now?"

There are, of course, a few big and powerful moments which should be experienced. But these are fairly rare and are sometimes frightening. The small and still moments of life also have a great purpose.

A Spot

Stake out an area three feet square or even smaller. For just five minutes a day you and a young child sit in stillness and look at that square. Accept everything, and do not talk during the experience. Afterward share what you have seen and felt. At first there will be some resistance from both of you. Then gradually there will be a sense of awareness and identification with what is there. Do this for about two weeks.

Even an older child benefits from lying on the ground for a period of time and looking out into space to get a sense of what is there.

The great cycle of life and death should be experienced in

ways which are appropriate to the child. One of the best preparations again has to do with a tree, but this time one which blooms and bears fruit.

Cycles
Each year the child should be taken to the tree to experience the blooming period, the period of leafing, the time when the fruit is produced, and the period of dormancy. The tree's cycle serves as a framework later for discussion about our own life cycle, including the paschal mystery, the liturgical year, the ebbing and flowing of friendships, the evolving and provisional nature of life.

The failure to have this rhythm is one of the problems of early spiritual growth, where everything is seen in a more linear fashion by the child, and some teachers. We should not expect one spiritual blooming after another forever. We must bear fruit, and from time to time we must be dormant.

An important lesson to be taught is the need to accept many aspects of life rather than to attempt to control or eliminate them, as is the American tendency. It is a simple but important lesson, for example, to train a child that when the house is chilly you put on a sweater rather than running to turn up the thermostat. This has a direct relationship to the spiritual life. On the one hand there is an awareness of a situation and a personal response to it. The alternative is simply to find a solution which eliminates the problem. The quest for a push-button spirituality is often a problem during adolescence and young adulthood. This fundamental difference of approach has been described in many religious traditions. There is a Buddhist tale which concerns two monks walking along a very rough road. They have been on it for a long time. One monk says, "If they covered this road with leather, it would certainly make traveling much easier." The other monk responds, "I think if I covered my feet with leather, it would be enough." The first talks about what "they" ought to do and the other takes personal responsibility. The first, in effect, does not wish to be aware of any force outside of his own comfort. The other is beginning to harmonize with life.

Step 3. *Awe*

In a classical work, Rudolph Otto describes the basis of all religious attitudes as the experience of the "holy," which is the "mysterium tremendum et fascinans," that is, the mystery which both attracts with its fascination and disturbs with its overwhelming power.[1]

Awe is an increasingly rare experience in American life. Our youth are quite blasé. They have seen everything there is to see in movies, which are frequently gross in attempts to impress youthful audiences. When all else fails, there are drugs. The desired effect is not to be open to awe, but, quite the contrary, to be unflappable and cool. The temptation to find a super-cool way of impressing the kids only increases the problem.

The Greek word "ek-plesso" is used in the Gospels to mean astonished, amazed, spellbound, awestruck—that a deep impression has been made. Interestingly, this word appears only in the Synoptic Gospels of Matthew, Mark and Luke. It does not appear in the Gospel of John, which is in many ways a smooth, we might even say "cool," picture of Jesus. In John nothing flaps Jesus; nothing is surprising to him. But in the other Gospels, awe is an essential part of the message.

A reference in Mark takes place at the beginning of Jesus' public ministry:

> They went as far as Capernaum, and as soon as the sabbath came he went to the synagogue and began to teach. And his teaching made a deep impression [*ek-plesso*] on them, because, unlike the scribes, he taught them with authority (1:21–22).

A similar reference in Matthew (7:29) comes at the end of a passage which indicates that Jesus has established himself at Capernaum and recites the essence of his teachings about how to live, culminating in what we term the Sermon on the Mount. This section includes the Beatitudes, the Sermon on the Mount, the Lord's Prayer and various principles such as the Golden Rule. In Luke (4:31) we also find the statement placed near the beginning of the Galilean ministry.

The overall image conveyed in all three Gospels is a sense

of awe. Here is someone quite out of the ordinary. The message of Jesus makes a "deep impression." We on our part have to leave the door open to the message. More and more in our modern world we are attempting to close the door to any type of depth experience. It is in early childhood that we should begin the practice of leaving that door open, even though it may be unused for long periods of time. A young child will be able to accept deep impressions which are out of the ordinary. Our function as Christian educators is to support that process.

When the child is young there is a need for many moments of awe. As we will discuss in the comments on "stillness" this is something to be practiced many times each year of a child's life. There should never, under any circumstance, be deception or trickery. If we expect the child, for example, to enter into the magic engendered by a trip to Santa, then we too must be willing to stand in awe of this old fellow and enter into the moment.

The opportunities for very young children in our families to experience surprise and awe are often associated with the first Christmas tree and family holidays. Occasions which bring about this reaction should never be slighted.

A child is naturally awed if he or she is in an environment that does not take everything for granted and one in which the adults are willing to admit that they do not know everything. One of the most important memories that people consistently recall as they attempt to reconstruct their spiritual history is the awe of being alone or with a loved adult in a special and holy place.

The Hopi Indian culture encourages its children to approach the spiritual life with awe. The Hopi have assumed that all children will, sometime between six and eight years old, have to be cured of their "coolness." There is one major initiation for both boys and girls. The children have been spending several evenings in a still and quiet position with their feet on a ledge and their knees under their chin. On the fourth day they are taken for Kachinyungta, the Kachina Society ritual. Observers of a ceremony taking place around 1914 related that young boys and girls were taken to the kiva clothed only in blankets. Each child in turn was led out to participate in gentle rituals, such as stepping through hoops of feathers and being blessed with bunches of corn, which were intended to encourage their growth. This was all carried out in a graceful liturgy presided over by the Kachina chief. Then suddenly and without warning three horrible-looking Kachinas burst onto the scene. Two of them carried whips in each hand and struck out unceasingly at anything in sight. They were painted black with white spots. Their masks had horns with bulging eyes and huge teeth. The third Kachina was their mother and was even more terrifyingly attired. Over the protests of adult sponsors each child was brought forth and whipped four times. The kiva was now pure chaos, with people jumping around and screaming.[2]

That night the children's hair was washed with yucca suds, a ceremony of deep religious significance. They then received their adult names from their godparents. Obviously, the Hopi were not concerned about childhood trauma. Yet I suspect that few have ended up on the psychiatrist's couch. An interesting point on the initiation is that one of the lessons to be learned concerns the inability of even the Kachina chief, who is father of them all, to protect them. This teaches that part of growing up is to be unprotected amongst surprises.

A smaller scale but equally impressive Hopi ceremony concerns "monster Kachinas" who bring justice to disobedient and unruly children. At one time the practice was handled in one village by a group of Kachinas making their way through the cold winter night. They stood before each house, called out any child known for his disobedience, and solemnly listed his offenses. Symbolically the child offered some little "tribute" in retribution. This was politely refused as insufficient. The young offender was undressed and splashed with cold water. While shivering in the icy weather he was warned to listen more carefully in the future to the instructions of his parents.[3]

Do these practices demonstrate the primitive nature of the Hopi, reveal a sadistic streak, or perhaps demonstrate that some of the adults have severe control problems concerning their children? No, the Hopi are quite legitimately called the "People of Peace." They are deeply spiritual. There is a remarkable loving relationship between the generations which has withstood the onslaught of an alien culture better than most other Indian cultures. Furthermore, there is a certain psychological maturity among the Hopi which has impressed most visitors. In searching for some explanation for these seemingly harsh practices we begin with the fact that the Hopi take their spirituality and religion very seriously. The major concern is the adult life of the child. They simply do not want to take a chance that a boy or girl will grow up to be an adult lacking in spiritual awe, for such a person will be spiritually hollow and persist in childish ways.

A similar concern is found in the training of young Zen monks. Even though these students are no longer children, some of the principles are applicable. The "dokusan" is the daily consultation with the spiritual master or "roshi." During this time the master gives to each student a koan, that is, an irrational problem which can be resolved not by the mind [right hand] but only through deep experience [left hand]. It is a means by which a young monk can "break through his small ego, to become aware of his real self." This is not always a pleasant situation. There has been formalized what is known as "busshin-gyo," which is translated sometimes as "great compassion." It happens at times that a monk who has been unable to get outside of his "small ego" does not want to go to see the master. The elder monks take him by force and deposit him before the master. This is "busshin-gyo." In other words, out of compassion a monk will not be allowed to remain in his exiled state. There is too much at stake, for eventually the persistent monk will be able to reach the state of awareness, "kensho," in which he transcends all his difficulties and finds himself resting in the hands of Buddha.

We must educate children to expect the unexpected and to be open to it.

Step 4. *Stillness*

I prefer the word "stillness" to "silence" or "quiet." These latter words have a connotation of the absence of noise. An attempt to get into a noiseless state can become quite active. "Stillness," on the other hand, conveys a sense of peace despite the noise, such as the calm within the eye of the storm. Associated with this concept is the spiritual attitude referred to as "detachment" or the freedom to transcend our desires and compulsions.

The Eagle

An image of stillness is that of an eagle flying high in the sky. Through stillness, we, like the bird, are able to launch ourselves and to experience this kind of freedom from all of the busyness which is keeping us earthbound.

The Clay Pot

We can also learn from a potter making a clay vase. The vase is formed on a flat spinning board. The process begins by putting the clay into the center. If the clay is off to the side, we are always fighting the movement of the board. This also often happens in life. We have one activity after another and we frantically try to get them all together. If, on the other hand, the clay is placed in the center of the board, then all that the potter has to do is to hold his or her hands in place and the same movement which was so disruptive before now simply provides the power by which the clay is shaped. The difference is that the clay is now "centered." To put it another way, there is now a "still point," that is, an unmovable point in the very center of the busyness. The spiritual lesson drawn from this illustration in Eastern and Western spiritual groups is that we must have that still point in the middle of our lives.

At the beginning and the end of Jesus' ministry there are strong references to still points in life. We start with the time alone in the wilderness.[4] We are told of interior conflicts as Jesus was tempted by Satan. The most poignant quiet in the New Testament is at the other end of the story in the Garden of Gethsemane. Jesus revealed: "My soul is sorrowful to the point of death" (Mt 26:37). We watch his depression and sorrow grow[5] and then observe Jesus regain his inner strength and meet the final ordeal with serenity. Between the wilderness and the garden there were other examples when he would "go off to someplace where he could be alone and pray" (Lk 5:16).

Stillness and prayer can be part of the same process, as will be demonstrated in Chapter 11. What is recommended here is not necessarily prayer, but simply an attitude of calm. Stillness is not an unnatural state for a child. The time in the womb was certainly a time when we lived the adage to "be still and know."

First Prayer
Working with an infant, it is helpful to place the child on a parent's lap (facing outward) as the adult prays or reflects. The relaxation and serenity of the adult will communicate from the parent's body to the child. Ideal places are in church, in front of a fireplace, in a quiet garden with not too many distractions, or in a special little corner where you and your child have had nice times together.

A foster godparent who has related extensively to abused youngsters over the years has followed this procedure with young children. She was surprised to find that boys and girls as old as ten or eleven would regularly ask to be held and seemed to truly benefit from this quiet time.

When children are in one of the very active phases of development the problem is often to slow them down enough to have a quiet moment. Some type of art experience will often be of assistance.

Mandala
The mandala is simply a circular drawing used in some schools of meditation as an aid for focusing. Round art is a common religious experience in all cultures. We value the "Rose Windows" of our cathedrals. The procedure is simply to provide a blank sheet of paper and some crayons. Encourage the child to look at the paper for just a moment and to "draw something which is circular and has a center." Very soon, in most circumstances, he or she will become lost in the process.

Once, while I was serving as a consultant to the Las Vegas Juvenile Court, I had with me a group of teenage boys with a reputation for quick tempers and violent reactions. I had encouraged them to draw mandalas as a means of slowing down their rhythms. They had been at it for just a few minutes when a wild and antagonistic group of boys broke into the room. There was a lot of name-calling and challenging. My group continued with their mandalas without saying a word. Soon the whole room had calmed down. After a while the others quietly left. This demonstrated to me the tremendous hunger for stillness which exists especially in active children.

Meditation for children is becoming popular, but it is still rare. It is, however, a good practice to encourage, individually or in small groups, especially when children are young. Meditation is the practice of closing the active phase of life to allow ourselves to become receptive to things we do not control. It is giving our active mind something simple with which to play. Meditation is not necessarily a spiritual practice. It can be self-improvement of one sort or another, or to reduce stress. Meditation can be a quiet way of reaching stillness, but it can also be intellectual, reflective, emotional or even physical. There are many popular books which give examples of how to experience these various dimensions.[6] What follows is simply one possible suggestion.

Breathing

If possible it would be well to have the training period with more than one youngster, so that the child does not think that he or she is being bombarded with adult attention and even manipulation. Begin in a quiet setting where there will be few interruptions. Provide something on which to focus, such as a candle.

Sitting cross-legged on a pillow is rather natural for children. They should be encouraged to sit in a straight position, whether on a pillow or a chair. Although there is dispute on the point, I find it best to have young children close their eyes. Begin by simply asking them to listen. Direct them to listen to the sounds in the room and the noise outside the room and the sounds of their own breathing. Do not get too involved with the sounds; just let them come in one ear and go out the other.

After a few moments encourage the children to focus on their breathing: to become aware of the air as it comes in and as it goes out. Become aware of the process of breathing itself. Encourage them to become aware of each breath and how the air travels through their body.

Gradually, encourage them to focus on the process of exhaling. As they push the air out they should push all of the air out. Point out that the air comes naturally to them. The emphasis is upon exhaling slowly and continually. Help them be aware of the downward motion in their body as they exhale.

In the beginning they can be kept at this exercise for only a few minutes. It can be considerably longer as they gain more experience. They should be brought very gently out of the experience. Have them again focus on the candle and then make a slow re-entry into other activities.

In both the mandala and the meditative experience it would be good to have some kind of quiet activity following. Few experiences are better than a quiet walk, either alone or with someone else, where we use our senses to become more aware of what is around us and to appreciate the serenity in our spiritual life.

10. A Program
for Spiritual Growth: Knowing

This chapter contains Steps 5 through 7. All three of these steps use the concept of "knowledge." This word often means a familiarity with facts. Here it is used in a broader sense. The original Greek meaning of "idiot" ["idiotes"] had nothing to do with mental deficiency. It meant a "private person," that is, one who did not share in the "public philosophy" or concerns about the ultimate meaning of life. John Courtney Murray made a contemporary definition:

> The idiot today is the technological secularist who knows everything. He is the man who knows everything about the organization of all the instruments and techniques of power that are available in the contemporary world and who, at the same time, understands nothing about the nature of man or about the nature of true civilization.[1]

The knowledge we are hoping to encourage in our children is the enlightenment that will enable them to come to a true understanding of their faith, their world and themselves.

Step 5. *Know Yourself*
"Who am I?" is a question appropriately asked in childhood. If it is not answered during childhood, it will remain a question in adult life.

In the beginning we learn from and perhaps identify with our environment. This, connected with certain instincts that come with us all, seems to serve us well as infants. It is the next stage of awareness that presents a problem.

For our most ancient ancestors there was no difficulty. When we were hunters there was much to do. If our family or community were to eat we had to labor hard. The child quickly found a place in this utilitarian world. And later, in the more sophisticated world of agriculture, there was perhaps even more of a place for the child. We learned to delay our rewards. We worked hard in the spring plowing and planting so that we might get a good harvest in the autumn. There was much to be done at all times. A sense of natural rhythm assisted us in discovering our place.

But as we began to urbanize we became more removed from natural cycles. Everyone had to ask "Where do I fit in?" and "Where is my place?" or, to put it more simply, "Who am I?"

In the beginning days of this century we more or less conspired to tell a child, "You are what I want you to be." This tended to make it difficult for them in later life. Many adults found that, separated from the family, they had trouble finding themselves. Even after parents were long dead, adults recreated a parental image to which they kept on answering. Spiritually, this is complicated by the fact that "God" and "parents" often tend to become confused images.[2]

As the twentieth century wore on we saw the pendulum swing in the opposite direction. Today many parents are more or less dependent on their children to answer the question, "What kind of a parent can I be?" Children are largely calling the shots as far as family relations are concerned. However, this situation in no way assists the child in answering the question, "Who am I?" In a crude way the answer can be picked up from television, rock singers, other children, movies and the like. In the long run such answers are not very satisfying.

When we fear our children, we tend to pamper them. There is a growing fear of adolescent violence, especially in the cities, and an increasing tendency to keep children happy in any way possible so as to reduce the possibility of some kind of revolt. We therefore contribute to a neurotic condition which Alfred Adler observed and warned about as early as 1936:

Extreme discouragement, continuing doubt, hypersensitivity, impatience, exaggerated emotion and phenomena of retreat, and physical and psychic disturbances showing the signs of weakness and need for support are always evidence that a neurotic patient has not yet abandoned his early-acquired *pampered lifestyle*. These show that a patient endowed with a comparatively small degree of activity, and not possessing sufficient social interest, has pictured to himself a world in which he is *entitled* to be first in everything.[3]

It should be pointed out, however, that Adler feels that the "pampered lifestyle" is basically the creation of the child, though its formation is frequently aided by others. It often arises in an environment of abuse and neglect as well as in over-indulged children.

Helping a child with self-knowledge is delicate in today's suspicious world. It is good to start early when there is a strong feeling of mutual trust.

The Task of the Parent

This is an opportunity to take out a moment to acknowledge the tremendous responsibility of parents in our age. If we made a "job description" of what it took to be a parent at this point in history, and if we happened to find anyone who was qualified, that person would probably not have the courage to take the position. First, there is all the normal training of walking, toilet, grooming, and eating. Then there are the increasingly difficult social interactions with others and the resulting need for ethical training that is keenly felt by Christian parents. There are then the medical and health needs, together with physical concerns and sports. Dating, sexual confusion, and emotional development start early. In addition we must face school and all the learning problems that go along with it. This is complicated by a growing frustration with the educational system.

As if this were not enough, we have the whole interior facet of life. When it comes to religious matters there is the sense of church etiquette—behaving in church, basic knowledge of and respect for the sacraments, and some training for the future.

And, then, in these pages is one more burden—spiritual growth. But even the most harassed parent knows that in the absence of spiritual growth many other problems will be intensified.

Personal History

A child tends to handle a deep quest with a disarming lack of emotion. A trivial question may be followed in the same tone by a matter of great significance. We are often not sure what is being said. You may recall the old joke about Johnny who asked his mother, "Where do I come from?" She responded with a complicated and full statement concerning the birth process and went on to discuss sexual responsibility. Johnny listened patiently, and thanked his mother. On his way out the door he said, "Sam says *he* comes from Omaha."

We should be careful not to give children more than they are seeking. Often we are loaded with answers and simply waiting for an appropriate opportunity to unload. We can smother the child with an overdose of information.

Being able to answer the "Who am I?" question requires that children have a good sense of their own personal history. The spiritual aspect of this will be shown in Stage 7, "Knowing Our Place in the Story of Life." In this present stage the personal history includes at least three elements.

(1) *Family History:* The child should frequently be reminded of his or her relationship with the members of the extended family. Most important is the transmittal of family stories and tales of what it was like when grandmother was a child, or when Uncle Jack was a farmer. The child begins to feel a part of the lore of the family as it evolves.

(2) *Physical History:* Records should be kept of all the significant physical facts. Height is important to a child. If possible there should be a scale drawn on a tree or a door where the child is measured at a birthday. I have found that even teenagers like to continue this practice. To a lesser extent there should be records kept about weight and other matters with which the child should be periodically acquainted to develop a sense of how he or she is growing. There should be an appreciation of

both the changes taking place and the ongoing stability within those changes.

(3) *Psychological History:* There should be frequent discussions about how there have been changes in outlook and attitude. For example, there probably were things which once frightened the child that do not anymore. Perhaps there were important frightening dreams or things that were emotionally satisfying which have now changed.

There should be a number of joint projects regularly in which the child is performing a constructive and needed part. Of course there should be good work habits and chores in the ordinary routine of family life. But of equal importance are the special family events which stand out in a child's mind. In those events his or her contribution to the enterprise should be obvious. It is more important than having fun. A family camping trip is pleasant, and certainly playing while mother fixes breakfast is more fun than going to get water from the creek. But it is being sent to get the water and watching that water find its place in the activities of the family that the child will remember. It is the sense of contribution that enhances the feeling of belonging and which allows the "Who am I?" question to be asked without triggering deep insecurity.

"This Is Me"

There is an artist inside each of us. To liberate that artist we must distract our mental and emotional controller. The basic process is to get lost in an art experience. This is fairly natural for young children. Start with a sheet of paper and pastels or crayons and encourage the child to be quiet.

One method requires two sheets of paper. Take the first sheet and have the child close his or her eyes and make simple movements in the air without touching the paper. Now, let the hand come down on the paper. Make circles, crosses, curves, straight lines or whatever other motions occur. One motion will begin to feel very right, and this one will begin to be repeated. When this happens ask the child to open his or her eyes and see what he or she has been doing.

Then take another sheet of paper and encourage the child to simply begin to draw on it in any way he or she wishes. Do not encourage them to perform for you. Avoid judgmental statements, such as "Oh, what a pretty picture!" The idea is to attempt to get the children to identify with what is in front of them. Let them tell you what they feel but avoid analysis of what it symbolizes. If there is a house in the picture then the child can tell you what it is like to be a house, or what the house wants to do. And EVERYTHING that comes out has to be accepted by you. The process is not one of gaining insight or information, but of allowing a person's wholeness to develop. These experiences are like a thermometer in knowing ourselves. Even though it perhaps cannot be put into words, they can at least experience what they are doing and who they are at that moment.

Step 6. *Knowing Others*

At the first mention of interpersonal relations among children in religious circles we are usually hurled into the important but quite distinct area of "moral education." Let us take up this issue first.

The Development of Conscience

In our often valueless world, we naturally worry about instilling values in our children. This is a difficult task for parents and religious educators. As one recently put it:

> We who have to present the Christian view on any of these topics know how carefully and painfully we have to steer a course between sounding "too corny and old fashioned" and watering down the Christian demands.[4]

One way out of this dilemma has been to teach what is sometimes termed *value clarification,* that is, setting out a number of conflict type situations and using these as a way of clarifying a child's attitude toward moral issues, especially as they relate to conduct toward other people. This process heightens awareness and is a springboard to discussions about matters of right and wrong.

Traditionally, all of our approaches to moral education stem from an application of *norms*. That is, we have a major premise, such as "The Ten Commandments say 'Thou shalt not kill.' " There is then a minor premise, "Engaging in war is killing." And we arrive at a conclusion, "To engage in war is therefore wrong." One cannot fault any part of such reasoning. The difficulty is that children, and perhaps all of us, do not actually follow this kind of process in the development of conscience.

From the children's point of view, such tremendous inconsistency often exists in adult conduct that they do not really take our logic seriously. For example, a child may listen to a religious education teacher talking about how we as Christians have to do everything we can to help the starving children in Africa. Later as the child is waiting for her parents to pick her up in the parking lot, she hears the chairman of the parish fund-raising drive indicating that they almost have the necessary $100,000 to put in a new cafeteria in the parish hall. She is naturally confused. To her the religious education teacher and the respected adult in the parking lot are both "the Church," as indeed they are. A child tends to resolve such matters by simply discounting both positions.

The conscience of a pre-adolescent child is usually the conscience of the family. We reinforce this by indicating to a child that "we do not hit our brothers in this family." Young children do not experience themselves as moral free-agents.[5] In general we put the cart before the horse. Conscience formation is a life response to our awareness of God and God's will. For the pre-adolescent the central emphasis should be upon developing that awareness of God.

I and Thou

This stage of "knowing others" is not a discussion of moral education. There is an entirely separate dimension of the interpersonal among children, and that is for children to know themselves, and to know God they have to develop a view of life which admits to the possibility that other people actually do exist, that they are not the total center of the universe!

The problem of "knowing others" is influenced by overlaying social problems. Following World War II there was a growing tendency for us to become "organizational" people. Our individuality was being drowned in the larger and larger organizations which we encountered in governmental, educational, religious and commercial bureaucracies. We tended to identify ourselves only by our practical functioning in life. "Who are you?" was usually interpreted to mean "What do you do?" and was answered in terms of a person's occupation. The thrust of humanistic psychology in the mid twentieth century was to combat what seemed to be a situation of serious rejection of our individuality. Christianity, regrettably, was often seen as part of the problem. In 1961 Carl Rogers observed:

> When men in the past have asked themselves the purpose of life, some have answered, in the words of the catechism, that "the chief end of man is to glorify God." Others have thought of life's purpose as being the preparation of oneself for immortality. Others have settled on a much more earthy goal—to enjoy and release and satisfy every sensual desire. Still others—and this applies to many today—regard the purpose of life as being to achieve—to gain material possessions, status, knowledge, power. Some have made it their goal to give themselves completely and devotedly to a cause outside of themselves—such as Christianity, or Communism.[6]

Rogers was one of the most influential and careful researchers in humanistic psychology. The state of affairs referred to above was seen as denial of personhood. Over and against this he succinctly put what was to become the humanistic agenda in the next decade:

> The best way I can state this aim of life, as I see it coming to light in my relationship with my clients, is to use the words of Søren Kierkegaard—"to be that self which one truly is."[7]

Rogers believed that, for various reasons, we were not attempting to be ourselves or to become ourselves. Rather we were becoming facades of ourselves. These facades were painfully and unhappily maintained at great cost to ourselves, and prevented us from becoming fully functioning human beings. He was suggesting a way out of the hell of the faceless, lonely crowd. Men and women by the thousands responded by placing "becoming a person" on the top of their life agendas.

Of course the abuse of this humanistic attitude led to the more grotesque manifestations of the "me generation" in which basically nobody but *me* counts. Now there is a jerky swing back to a more balanced position. We should recognize, however, that it was only a short time ago in psychological circles that the "You do your thing and I do my thing" philosophy was prevalent, and confusing to those who longed for a more cooperative world.

How is all this psychological and theological theory applied when we face little Debbie or little George some morning? The basic issue is: Can they see that each other exists? Of course there are radical confrontations. When Debbie hits George, George realizes that Debbie is something to be reckoned with, but the emphasis here is on *thing*. Debbie can be seen as a source of annoyance. Furthermore, parents can require that the children be polite to each other and to adults, but this may result because the children desire reward or fear punishment—in which case, again, the child simply looks to others as potential sources of interference. There is a vital issue in Carl Rogers' approach which is important in the spiritual development of young children. We must realize the significance of what we might call "genuineness" or, in more traditional psychological jargon, "congruence." What is being described is the connection between experience, awareness and communication. For example, it is tempting to play the game and go along with the child who simply wants the attention received from an imaginary ailment. But the truly kind thing to do is to insist on the child getting directly what he or she is moving for indirectly.

Those who have worked with severely emotionally disturbed children are perhaps super-sensitive to this issue, because these youngsters often have such a high degree of incongruity. Personal experience can be absorbed in a complex fantasy within carefully built and controlled walls. At times there is an almost total lack of awareness. It is somewhat like being trapped in an elaborate sand castle of your own making with the tide coming in. We do them no favor by joining them in the trap.

The young baby is almost always genuine. There is a high congruence between experience, awareness, and communication. In later life our most common incongruence is usually denying feelings. We might be especially angry about something but feel that we ought not to be, and so therefore we will indicate that we are not at all angry but simply pointing out the logic of a situation. We may put on a facade of a smiling person, but others looking at the rest of our body may observe a tense or hostile person. We may carefully learn the vocabulary of a warm person to cover a cool reserve or shyness.

Our task as Christian educators is to encourage in every possible way that a child be authentic, the principle being that the more genuine the child the more he or she is open to reality and the less likely to attempt to put other people into carefully manipulated positions on a chess board of life.

Some kind of spiritual leap or "paradigm shift" is necessary for most children.

Act As If

In this part of our century we have become fascinated by Mother Teresa of Calcutta's simple statement that she sees God in the people she is helping. Some of us might be able to actually do the same thing. But most of us would have to apply another helpful principle of humanistic psychology: to "act as if" it were true. If "I act as if I see Jesus in everyone I meet," I will begin to change my life in a constructive way. This is a practical tool for catching young children's imagination, especially if a parent does the same thing, say for half a day. To the child it can be a game, but a very constructive one.

Is this process contrary to what has just been said about the necessity for genuineness in all relationships? No, because there is an openness about what the people are doing and why they are doing it. In this sharing with the child and the encouragement that goes along with it new frontiers can be opened up on what it means to have a relation with another person.

We have in some way to translate into the child's language the concepts of the Jewish philosopher Martin Buber.[8] To Buber there are two basic ways of looking at the world, the "I-Thou" approach and the "I-It." Unlike Rogers, Buber, who wrote in the post World War I era, did not find much of an issue with the denial of the "I." He was concerned about how the "I" perceived everything else. Now, after a time of denying self we are swinging back, and Buber's concerns become again relevant for today, equal to the attitudes of those psychologists who desire to see the individual human potential more fully developed. To Buber we basically "experience" another person as a thing when we are concerned about what that person can do for us or to us. The person is an "it" as any other object we experience. The opposite is to "stand in relation to" an individual. In today's vocabulary the term "encounter" would probably be proper. I do not sit in a personal command center pushing buttons. Rather, I am somehow dancing around the universe in a relationship with another human being. I realize that every second we are together we are having an effect on each other.

In the "I-It" situation I can predict and control what will happen. It "hangs together in space and time." Whereas in the "I-Thou" relationship we do not hang together in space and time and there is a great deal of uncertainty. To translate it to familiar psychological concepts, the "I" of the "I-Thou" is a person, as distinct from the "I" of the "I-It," which is simply an "ego" concerned about its relationship to other egos. It is conscious of its separateness, and in fact may be desirous of maintaining that separateness. There are many purposes for "I-It" relationships. But in the "I-Thou" relationship "the purpose of the relation is the relation itself"—touching the Thou. As soon as we touch a thou we are touched by a breath of eternal life:

> What do we have to pay for this "I-Thou" relationship? What has to be given up is not the I but that false drive for self-affirmation which impels man to flee from the unreliable, unsolid, unlasting, unpredictable, dangerous world of relation into the having of things.[9]

Our concern is for authenticity in the growth of our children, which means we must be concerned about the *things* in their lives. If they grow up in a world of things, where they can count on stimulating things (such as television), feeding things (such as mommy), laughing things (such as toy ducks)—*if* their entire world is filled with such things which are basically under their control—it is natural for them, as they experience other children and other adults, to simply treat them as things.

Recently there was a fantasy television program which described an electric grandmother, designed to be and look exactly as the child desired. This was found superior to the human types which were unpredictable, not always focused on the child, and died, causing unnecessary disturbance. It was chilling to discover how many viewers—child and adult—thought it was a great idea.

Training a child not to rely upon things is difficult in our materialistic society, but it is a spiritual necessity. Otherwise God becomes a thing. In later life, when the God-thing does not do what it is supposed to do, we toss it away with the toy duck, and settle down to the fact that in this whole universe the only real thing is *"me."* This can be a very lonely situation.

Step 7. *Knowing Our Place in the Story of Life*

One of our most important adult functions is to transmit the essence of life to the younger generation. This is a responsibility not limited to parents. We must all teach the child that he or she has a place in life.

The essence of any tribe's initiation of the young is that they know the story that has gone before. They can no longer act as if the world began when they were born. They must look beyond themselves and see the entire story. We have not done well in the Christian initiation process. The most important aspect of that process will always be the child realizing that on the one hand there is a lot more to life than his or her own individual existence, and also that each fits into the story as a unique individual. This task is especially difficult in today's world because we like to believe that things are always new and changing. A child can be initiated into this tribe of perpetual progress, but it does not seem to be a very satisfying process. It is more fulfilling for children to be initiated into the overall story of life and to know their beginnings and their ends.

This book tries to avoid giving tremendous details on how to do things. Detailed manuals of how to do this and that with your child have some serious drawbacks. The natural creativity that exists between people is often shoved aside as we respectfully listen to the experts. However, because I know this particular aspect is difficult, I would like to share with you a process which I used recently with some children in the fifth and sixth grades. A number of them came to a retreat with a parent. We were going through several of the stages reflected in this book, especially those where the parent's activities could be assisted by a program outside of the family. We came to the point in the retreat of talking about the story of life. What follows was a fairly spontaneous statement. This is not intended in any way to be a model. It reflects my own particular interests and confusions. It is included rather to encourage everyone to express the story of life in his or her own way.

Parents and children were sitting in pairs in a relatively large room. With my prompting, the parents began to instruct their own children, who were listening respectfully. They did not have much choice the way I set it up. The parent would tell first about the child's own personal history. There was a lot of warm humor in this. Then the family history was reviewed, going back as far as was practical. After this the children came together. They were on the floor directly in front of me. The parents were sitting in a circle behind them. And this is what I told them:

Your Place in the Story

You are part of a big story. It is the story of life itself. This story can be imagined as if it were a large river. The river is very wide and smooth at times, and at other times it is narrow, wild and rocky. Coming into the big river are many, many small streams. There is one stream for every person living today.

One of these streams is you. Your life started in the dark and warm space inside your mother. And after nine months you came out into the world. At first you didn't want to. In fact it took a lot of courage, perhaps the most courageous thing you will ever have to do in your life, to come into this world. For this was a very bright, noisy and scary world. Everything was new. Everywhere was color, sizes and shapes that were unusual to you. But you made it! You did a good job! People took care of you because you could not take care of yourself. They held you, they fed you, they dressed you, they washed you. And they began teaching you many things.

Then after a while you began to walk around. You discovered that there were other boys and girls in the world. And every day you were taught how to take care of yourself, how to have fun and find happiness, how to think and how to find God. Sometimes you did the right thing and everybody smiled. Sometimes you did the wrong thing and everybody frowned. But even after bad days there were always good days.

In a few years it became time for you to go to school. Now you were meeting more and more boys and girls. You were being taught, not only at home, but also at school, by teachers, and you learned about yourself, your family, your country, and your Church.

There is a story to your family, and you are part of it. You may have someone who is a mother or a father to you, or both, living with you. They were once a child like you. And some of the things they were taught by your grandparents they have now taught you. And some of those same things that you have been taught, you will teach other boys and girls. You are learning but you are also going to be a teacher.

Your country has a story, and you are part of that also. It was very hard in the beginning of our country. You have heard the stories of the pilgrims in the east and the pioneers in the west. We have always been a strong people. We made homes in a wilderness, and it was beautiful. But then we began to grow, and some things were not so beautiful anymore. There were problems of crime and poverty and pollution and war and other things. But we are still a strong people, and you and I must find a way to solve these problems.

Your Church has a story too. What is a Church? Is a Church the building where you go on Sundays? No. We call that a church, but that is not what I mean. Some of you have friends who go to other places on Sunday. We say, I am a

Catholic, or I am a Baptist, or I am Jewish. We all belong to different Churches, and some belong to none. Is this what I mean by Church? No, I don't mean these different groups.

The real meaning of the word Church is the whole of God's people—you and everyone else in the world. And through this Church God can touch us and be with us. Jesus has said that when even two or three of us gather in his name—in the name of all the people—he is with us. We are all God's people, and so let us call ourselves the people of God. And there is a story for the people of God, and you are part of it.

Remember, I told you the story of life was like a big river. The story of life is also the story of the people of God. Through God we learn what life is really about. Each of us is a stream, and we each flow into this big river. And so you are now a part of that story, because your little stream of life flows into the big river. It is very important for you to remember that you are a part of this story. Now, let us look at that big story, that story of life, that story of our people, that story of the people of God—your story.

In the beginning there was no earth. There were big storms stretching out across the heavens. And then somehow in the midst of those storms, our little planet began to form. Sometimes it would be very hot and steaming with volcanoes, and at other times it was very cold and covered with ice. We, the people, began in the sea, as tiny creatures. And after a long time we came out and walked upon the earth. We began to change until we became men and women. We lived in caves and we hunted.

After a while some of us began to grow our food and some of us became farmers. But we did not get along very well. We fought each other and we hurt each other. Those who were farmers and those who hunted or kept sheep did not trust each other. Then God began to make himself known to us. To some of us he made himself known just as you know him today. To others who lived in the high mountains to the north, or in the jungles to the south, or in the islands on the ocean, God made himself known in different ways, but it is the same God.

For you and for me and for those who came before us, one of the most important ways God made himself known in our story was through the Israelite people, whom we now call Jewish. They lived in the desert for many, many years. And because our brother Jesus was a Jew, you can say we are all Jews, and their story is part of your story. So it is that our people were wandering in the desert with their flocks of sheep, and they were a good people. They felt that God was with them. He had said to them, "You are my people and I am your God." In the quiet under the stars they learned to know the peace and quiet of God within them, and they were happy.

But there was trouble. There is always trouble in life. This time it was bad. The Jewish people ended up in Egypt as slaves. But then a great leader came, named Moses, and he led his people, your people, out of Egypt, and with God's help he rescued them and he brought them to their own land. God gave us laws and taught us how to behave, that we might have happiness, and be a good people.

And many, many years later, our people were again in slavery, but now it was a different kind of slavery. God wants us to be happy, but we had not lived as God wanted us to. We had made ourselves very unhappy, and we had lost our freedom. We were sad, because we had gotten ourselves in trouble again. People had kicked us around and said we were no good. Many of us were thrown out of society. We were sad because we were poor and hungry. Many of us were sick and blind and lame. We were sad because we all had to work hard and long and had very little to eat after each day. And, we were sad because we had no freedom. Other countries had conquered us. We could not see any way out, and we were sad because we were trapped. We were sad because there were so many rules that had been made that we were always breaking them. We were very, very unhappy.

And then Jesus came and walked among us. He was like the sun on a spring day. He healed us and he made us happy. He taught us that God loved us, and that God was our father, our mother and our friend. He taught us how to love each other. And through him we learned about the kingdom of heaven, and that we had the power to make this dream become real. We learned that the world was beautiful again. We had hope, and we were no longer sad.

Then our brother was tortured and murdered. And again we were alone and all was very black. It had been so good for a while, and now it was worse than ever.

But somehow we began to know that he had not really left us. Some saw him, and we knew that death had not stopped him. And what a joy your people felt! And then a great miracle occurred. The ordinary people who had followed Jesus around, like Peter the fisherman and his friends, had been very frightened to stand up. Somehow now they had great courage, and they stood up. Everything that Jesus had taught them they now taught others. They felt God inside them, and they felt God beside them. They spread the good news that all could be happy. They spread it throughout the world.

Now we knew for sure that Jesus had not been a failure. The story did not stop. It is still going on to this day. And we, you and I, are a part of it. For we now are the hands of God. You and I can make the world beautiful.

And the story will go on. In not too many years you will be grown, and some of us—myself, your parents, your teachers—we may be gone, but you will be here. We taught you, and you will teach other young people. So long as there are any of us Jesus will live and bring joy to the world!

And so, my little brothers and sisters, you see you are part of a very long story, which will go on and on, even after you.

Sometimes we have been lost, and sometimes you will be lost, and you will not know your way. You will forget where you are. But it doesn't matter. God will help you find your way again. He always does. Always remember, the world is different because you were born. Because you are here the world is a better place than it would have been without you. Do you remember that great river I told you about, that story of your people? It is going to flow on for a very long time, and you will always be a part of it as long as it flows.

After I had finished, the children got up and went to their parents. Together they quietly left the room. Each couple of parent and child walked and talked together.

11. A Program for Spiritual Growth: Encountering the Other

We have now come to what many see as the center point of spiritual growth—prayer. But there is an even more inclusive concept which is in the name of this chapter, "Encountering the Other." Why "Other"? Why not simply "God"? In some ways the word "God" itself is restrictive. It is a term we use to describe a mystery. Some Christian mystics distinguish between "God," an active phenomenon, and the "Godhead," which is characterized as a deep stillness. This latter dimension has been described in Eastern concepts as:

> Something formless yet complete
> existing before heaven and earth.
> Silent and limitless
> it stands alone and does not change.[1]

There is a practical problem about "God" as a term. When we say "God" it is difficult for children to escape a mental image which limits their experience. Surveys of young adults asked to describe how they pictured God consistently turn up such answers as "The Eye," "A kindly old man," "Really Big and Powerful," "Sweet smile and white robe," and "Like a neighbor." The image-building process is continued today despite rather consistent theological advice not to see God as an object and to be cautious about taking too literally the metaphor of God as a person. This is hardly new advice, for St. Paul says ours is a God "whom no man has seen and no man is able to see" (1 Tim

6:16).[2] But any parent knows that the child is going to concrete-
ly define any concept, and they will "see" God. It is not unusual, when we tell a youngster that we do not know what God
"looks like," to have the child volunteer to dispel our ignorance
by a complete description. The term "The Other" is suggested
as someplace in between the concrete and the abstract. With
some children it has been an agent in the development of a constructive provisional image. It also helps the adult recall that
God can be experienced whenever we step away from our preoccupation with ourselves.

The central focus of this chapter concerns prayer. The basic
recommendation is that adults should teach the approach to
prayer that they practice. This presents to the child a beginning
point from which to evolve his or her own approach through the
years. God loves to play with children. These moments of contact are all times of prayer, no matter what takes place. The fundamental problem is the adult's own problem with prayer, and
that is what we will concentrate on primarily. Let us consider
some basic assumptions.

Preliminary Considerations

1. The old definition of prayer as a "lifting up of heart and
mind" needs some modification. Prayer is an encounter with
God, who is often unknown, and most often not "up." The kingdom of God is within us, we are told in Luke's Gospel (17:21).
But even "within" presents some problems in light of new
knowledge about human development. The inner/outer spiritual
dichotomy is certainly arbitrary. What is described as "inner" is
often really imaginary or sentimental. But using the "inner" metaphor we can at least help a child appreciate that the God encountered in prayer is not "out there," and especially not "up
there." Rather there is some kind of small indefinable inside tick-
le. This elusive experience has to be affirmed by the adults in the
child's life.

2. It is also necessary to overcome our tendency to think of
prayer as "speaking to God." It is fruitful to have a child at a
very early age realize that he or she does not have to *do* any-

thing to be praying. Prayer is a gift of God, or, to put it another way, a grace from God. It is enough to listen or simply be quiet. It is not always easy for children to be quiet, but it is not nearly as hard as asking them to talk to someone whom they do not see.

3. Another preliminary point is that spirituality, especially prayer, develops like the common cold—it has to be caught from someone, usually the parent. Whatever an adult's approach to prayer, this is what should be taught to their children. The experience must be authentic. This raises a problem we like to ignore. It is not uncommon for today's adults to have trouble in praying. This is also true of all, even if they be members of the clergy or of religious communitites. The beginning step in teaching our children to pray is to learn how to pray ourselves. It is counter-productive for a parent or teacher to attempt to "train" a child in some prayer method which the adult does not regularly and effectively use. If we share our own personal process the child will somehow catch on and eventually be found by God. If we give children instead some kind of methodology, all that they will have is a method, and perhaps some associated good, but passing, feelings.

4. Some adults have been in an arid place spiritually for such a period of time that they basically have given up any hope of a flowering prayer life. Partly this attitude of "nothing-will-ever-happen" has to do with some rigid concepts of what it would take to have a "meaningful" prayer life. It has something to do with renouncing pleasure, embracing discipline, and being bored. Therefore, projecting their own fear of boredom onto their children, they eschew any methods that are not entertaining and of short duration. A recent author on prayer capsulated what is undoubtedly the attitude of many adults—that "we need to train people in simple, and direct ways of meditating, since most parents and teachers probably don't have the time or money to complete an extensive spiritual training program." This attitude reflects that any help that we are ever going to get has to be from an extended course on spirituality with concepts which are hard to fathom. If we indeed believe that prayer is an encounter with God, it is difficult to find anything that would be more important in our lives. Therefore the fact that we "do not

have the time or money" to get into it indicates another assumption—that events such as courses probably are not going to do anything for us anyway.

We adults are starving, yet we only desire to satisfy ourselves with pleasant little snacks. Fortunately, children, unless trained otherwise, can be very patient and even long-suffering when it comes to prayer.

5. Although the discussion that follows will be mostly concerned with individual non-verbal prayer, it is important to emphasize that verbal prayer and common prayer, especially the liturgical prayer of the Church, are of enormous importance to a child. But such objective experiences are, in many cases, more properly the subject matter of religious education.

Formal prayers can be traditional or contemporary; they can be public or private. Public formal prayers range from Eucharistic liturgies to small group meditations. The private aspects usually occur in the home—grace before meals, night-time prayers, moments associated with yearly festivals and events, and times of crisis in the family. These are important and should be encouraged, but they often do not relate to spiritual growth directly. They have more direct relation to the child's developing a sense of community. Indirectly, there are some significant aspects; kneeling, being quiet, and other physical disciplines are good for the child if not oppressive. Furthermore, little silent moments before, after and during such experiences do enable the child to be grasped by God and often produce rich memories in later life.

Formal prayers should be seen in a category by themselves. They do not have to be in a baroque style. They may start with folk music, go to exciting images and fantasies, even have audiovisual sections, brilliant commentaries on Scripture, times of personal reflection with suggestions like "Now tell God how you feel," and an interchange of experience and encounter among the young participants following the session. On the surface this certainly differs a great deal from the Tuesday night novenas, but it is nonetheless formal. The relationship is not simply between God and the child, but between God (hopefully), the leader, and the child. There are attempts to stimulate particular affective or intellectual states through the use of various media.

Such experiences should be approached with caution, even though they may be enjoyable.

In the area of spiritual growth these verbal and common prayers can also be important, but usually not in the way intended. Often they are preparations for prayer, that is, a means of quieting down. They may be an experience of other steps in this program, such as "awe" or "knowing our place." We must, in truth, admit total ignorance of what goes on when a child kneels down to say prayers at night or goes to a Sunday service. Nonetheless, whatever is going on is probably important.

There is also the issue of religious literacy. Young and dynamic catechists with whom I have worked frequently have only grudgingly cooperated with my request that children be taught the normal prayers and prayer forms of the religious history. Again, however, this is in a different realm from the more intimate development of spiritual growth.

6. Today we have a severe problem with terminology. Workshops on prayer are popular. Almost every leader or author has a unique way of describing his or her experience. There is little attempt to relate terms to other approaches. For example, the common term "meditation" can mean such widely differing things as (1) an emptying out of all images and sensations, (2) a quieting down of the emotions as preparation for prayer, (3) active intellectual reflections on some particular point of theology or Scripture, (4) a process in which we both talk and listen to God—and undoubtedly many other things as well. Also, terms like "centering" which has a poetic use in Eastern religion have now become either (1) a rather technical term describing particular approaches to prayer which have existed for some time in Western spirituality, or (2) a preparatory period of relaxation before one enters into the prayer experience. I propose to avoid as many "technical" terms as possible in this chapter and to seek a more practical concept which hopefully could be absorbed into whatever framework a person is currently using.

Teaching Children What You Know
As pointed out above, the first principle in teaching children to pray is to initiate them into the approach you use personally.

The transmission of the skill for being in touch with the divine will take place over a long period of time. Teaching prayer is never anything but sharing prayer. Aspects of a process may have to be more formally taught, but these should be kept to a minimum. It is essential that persons should never attempt to teach a child anything about prayer which they themselves do not presently practice.

But, as has already been discussed, we have a missing link or two in the prayer chain. For a host of reasons many people grew up in the mid-twentieth century with no meaningful prayer life and not much they could label as encounter with God. In recent years the problem has been much more openly discussed, but it is still difficult for many to admit that they have difficulty. There is in fact a not uncommon rather hopeless feeling about prayer, leading some to forget about it through elaborate theological arguments or to simply accept an arid spiritual state. For others there is a virtual carnival of prayer methods, seminars, cassette tapes, books, lectures, and degree-granting programs springing up around the country. A large segment of America's young adults are interested in spirituality and prayer. But despite our growing armies of eager Christian spiritual directors, these young people quietly continue to turn to gurus and roshis of Eastern religion for nourishment. One reason is that at present we do not present a very convincing picture for those who are seeking authentic experience rather than methodology. For those who have trouble with prayer, and I believe this means everyone, the important thing is to be simple. Try for yourself some of the suggestions in this step. Those who admit to frustrations in the prayer experience can take encouragement from the monastic maxim: Attempting to pray is praying.

Theological Rules

We always have the opportunity of starting the prayer process anew. To a large extent it is necessary to forget about all the current furor and also the semi-official textbook teachings of the Church concerning interior prayer. These were based on concepts about people and God which are simply no longer held. The spirituality of the Protestant Reformation, reacting to the mechanical ritualism and superstition of the medieval Church, emphasized the personal relation between God and people in such a way that it often denied the communal aspects of the body of Christ. Ironically this actually exceeded the privatism of the medieval Church and, coupled with some rather wild emphases on personal mystic manifestations, made the whole area of prayer suspect to nervous churchmen. As a result, if a person could not express experience in terms of the theological notions of the day it was not believed to be real, and was perhaps even diabolic. There was an official theological developmentalism. The process was broken up into many stages and steps. You were not to go on to the next until you had successfully finished the previous one. There was also a great chasm emphasized between what the individual should attempt to do and what God would have to do himself in us. It is not an exaggeration to say that the churchmen of the time even attempted to organize God's own activity. Good Christians, fearful of being presumptuous, suffered in the strife between what was often a natural calling and the guidelines of their elders. Fortunately there were, as always, some spiritual delinquents who kept the flame alive and laid the foundation for today's spiritual renewal.

The Counter-Reformation's oppressive attempt to control the spiritual experience led to safe and bland approaches. As St. Teresa of Avila and many others have pointed out, there was also a great deal of human error and unnecessary pain in the process. About the seventeenth century we attempted to escape from the problem through increasing reliance on sentimental devotionalism.

New Thoughts

There is a growing tendency to view the methods and rules and practices of past centuries as a general expression of universal phenomena, but in specific terms which are only relevant to the particular conditions of that time and place.

When we look to the prayer of Jesus himself we find (1) simplicity, (2) confidence in the Father, (3) security, (4) communication, and (5) obedience, or more accurately a blending of wills. From a psycho-spiritual perspective we can appreciate the prayer of Jesus as an attempt at being who we really are. This has led theologians like Karl Rahner to define prayer as "What man really is in the depths of his being." But this is not enough; "inner" and "outer" experience must be bridged. Therefore, prayer "must be realized in a fundamental activity in time yet transcending time." At the root of the process we accept "the prime fact of being created." From our "longing for happiness" comes a "personal fulfillment" which is a person's commitment "to the transcendence of his own being." Through this self-awareness we say YES to our "call and destiny" and comprehend to some extent the impact of the existence of God in human existence.[3]

Such thoughts about prayer, although difficult at times to understand, are exciting. They need to be unfolded and given practical meaning through the ordinary life experience of Christian men and women. This is an important agenda for the coming decade.

Today, it is best for us to attempt to transcend past controversies over prayer and to look back to those times in the early Church when there was not a sharp line of demarcation between prayer life and social, physical, emotional and intellectual concerns. It is necessary to provide a child today with a natural continuum of experience which we very likely never received ourselves.

There is a great temptation to read about and attempt to do new things in which we are effectively a middleman between the person who wrote the book (including this one) and our child. This is not wise. If we are to guide, it is essential to remember the principle that we must share that which is meaningful to us personally. The child will pick up not only what we think we are conveying but a great deal more as well. Something in that process will be an enduring and authentic experience which in the long run will enable them to feel at home in their own Western spirituality. Just what that something is will never be known.

Responsive Prayer
In the other steps in this suggested program, suggestions have been made which encourage a sense of awareness and an

attitude of listening. Now we encounter God through a process of going out to meet someone who is coming to meet us.

Terms which have been used in the past, such as "mental prayer," are confusing. They have connotations of the intellectual or cognitive. Even the old term "interior prayer" can set up a false dichotomy between inner imagination and outer reality. A more neutral term like "response" is preferable in working with younger children.

Varieties of Prayer

There are many different approaches to *responding* to this coming together with "The Other." It can become confusing when we try to apply a small bit of wisdom gained from one approach to another reality. One issue concerns the use of mental images. On the one extreme we find those who advocated an encounter with God which is completely *lacking in images.* This is the position of such people as Dionysius the Areopagite, Evagrius, and many of the other desert monks and nuns. We are familiar with it today in Zen Buddhism. Their position is that God is not a thing—in other words, a "no-thing." If we are focused on any *thing,* even a concept like "Father," it is something that we ourselves are creating. At the other end of the spectrum is the acceptance of *images,* either coming from God in miraculous or natural ways, or produced by us. Teresa of Avila falls in this camp.

There are at least two variations on each of these poles. The imageless approach can be tending toward abstract *speculation,* such as Meister Eckhart and other German spiritual leaders of the fourteenth century. It can also be emphasizing the *affective* side of human nature (love, sorrow, etc.). This was true of the author of the *Cloud of Unknowing,* another fourteenth century text.

In the school making rich use of imagery with a cognitive tendency can be found such people as Ignatius of Loyola and his *Spiritual Exercises.* The emphasis on images coupled with warm emotion is furthered by Julian of Norwich and others.

And, of course, most spiritual masters do not fit comfortably into any one of these niches for all time, but it is helpful to see this distribution in order to resolve some differences in method which at times can be disturbing.

There are other relevant matters. First, what was the goal of the spiritual writer? For example, in the sixteenth century Ignatius of Loyola, caught up in the Counter-Reformation and the great need to revitalize the Church, put forth his *Spiritual Exercises* as a tool for helping to teach us how "to serve God." The focus is on a very practical prayer which would go hand in hand with the active ministry of the Church. In contrast, the fourteenth century monk, feeling himself in a more unified Christendom and focused on the "better part" in the Mary-Martha dichotomy, would, like the author of the *Cloud of Unknowing,* be much more concerned with "tasting God" rather than encouraging readers to "serve."

There are different approaches to the issue of method itself. The medieval monk, like some Buddhists, was really using a methodless method. This was associated with a tendency to, like their Zen counterparts of later times, strive toward a detached state which was to a large extent emotionless and lacking in intellectualism. Other spiritual masters were very method-oriented, especially after the Reformation. These were sometimes inclined toward a particular emotion or intellectual goal.

There was a definite difference in approach if the spiritual master was writing for people who lived in strong spiritual communities. Where the community was strong, the "community was the guru," as the Cistercian scholar Charles Dumont has put it. This is identical to the concerns of Zen as reflected in Joshu's comment:

> Before enlightenment,
>   chopping wood and carrying water.
> After enlightenment,
>   chopping wood and carrying water.

An individual who does not exist in the community environment tends to be subject to all sorts of additional deceptions, distractions and confusions, and is more in need of method and structure. Because the structures were cumbersome, much of the spirituality in the fractured community of the post-Reformation world degenerated into private, mechanical devotions.

Applying this latter observation to young children, we can appreciate an urgent need to give at least some attention to methodless approaches in the early years when a child is in a strong family community.

The Environment for Prayer

One of the most effective ways of guiding a child in prayer is to make sure that the child's community in the early years is a Gospel-oriented community. That is, children should experience from the family a life which resembles what they would have experienced had they been in the community of Jesus of Nazareth. This is an admittedly tall order in some ways, but in other ways it is an extremely practical approach.

If we can place children in a home community and ask ourselves every day "Have these children been treated as Jesus would have treated them?" and if a significant amount of the time we can say "yes," then those children are going to encounter the divine in that environment the same as they would have encountered it being with Jesus. And this is perhaps the most practical method for teaching prayer or the experience of God to children in the very first years of their lives.

Getting It Together and Sharing It

The process begins with the parent, foster godparent or teacher putting together his or her own prayer life and proceeding to share it. This is done by inviting children in a way appropriate to their age to participate in something which, it is obvious to them, is valued and appreciated by the adult. There is no way of short-cutting this process. Today, the prayer experience and preferences of adults are likely to cover a much broader spectrum than they would have thirty years ago. In addition to the traditional approaches, there have been strong tendencies toward Eastern or Near Eastern method (Buddhist, Zen, Hindu, Sufi, etc.). There are also many parents who have been enriched by charismatic prayer, and a significant number whose prayer life includes in some way the inner-focusing exercises inspired by depth psychology. Others may use "the centering prayer," meaning a modern rendition of concepts reflected in a number of places, including the *Cloud of Unknowing.* There are many who seek that indefinable sense of simply walking with God in natural settings.

The adult who transmits our spiritual tradition to a child has a responsibility to be aware of the historical position we current-ly occupy in the overall story of our people. To discover the ma-jor problem of prayer today we must look back on the 1950's. The American Catholic Church in this decade is accurately de-scribed by Jesuit historian James Hennesey as "a pervasive mor-alism" and "religious privatism in a professedly communitarian church," "long lines at Saturday afternoon and evening confes-sions" and "the willingness of churchmen . . . to legislate the ti-niest minutiae of church observance."[4] In other words we existed in a static universe where all the details had been deter-mined by a canon lawyer at some time in history. We were a judged people. This tends to create an overly individual ap-proach, as we are intent on saving ourselves from judgment. For many the unique essence of Catholicism was religious "privat-ism," an individual relationship with God, usually with a clerical mediator in the process. Devotional practices came close to the occult. Which of us has not stepped over into superstition and magic? The approach to the spiritual life was assumed to be highly individualistic, as we had the necessity of saving our indi-vidual souls.

In reaction to the past some progressive theologians have practically denied any personal avenue to the encounter with God. Wholeness in Christian life is to be found between these extremes. The movement flowing out of Vatican II, but not new with it, emphasizes the community and divine love in the place of the individual and divine justice.

It is important for us to guard against unconsciously devel-oping or reinforcing some ultra-traditionalist psychological atti-tudes in our children. Let us be cautious of four basic points:

1. Try to avoid dualism. "Soul" is not more real than "body." "Inner" is not superior to "outer." There are some ap-

proaches to spirituality which are so much on an inner plane, at least in the way of describing them, that they seem to deny any physical reality. We act as if the physical world is not really significant, and perhaps even evil.

2. Prayer does not separate us from the world. The individual encounter with God is not the only way God touches people. A spirituality which emphasizes only the personal and private relationship to God is likely to be ego-filled.

3. There should be a recognition that there is not "one way." There is no one true-for-all-time spirituality. In this regard care should be taken not to exclusively point prayer experience only in the direction of one divine attribute, such as Jesus alone, the Father only, or only life in the Spirit.

4. Individual spiritual experiences are not sufficient for a Christian life. To let God find us completely we must experience him also within a community. This does not only mean finding God in the sacrament of the Word and Eucharist but also in the evolution of the kingdom of heaven on earth. What goes on at a time of prayer must be related to our general life in all aspects. Prayer is not just a refreshing moment to be turned on and off like a TV series. Also, a moment of prayer is a means of sanctifying the ordinary events of everyday life.

5. All people are called to God. There is no spiritual elite. People who pray are not better or more loved by God than those who do not.

A Practical Approach

There are some general considerations which can be applied to all approaches to prayer. What is written below is primarily designed as practical suggestions for parents or foster godparents, but could also be adapted for teachers and pastors.

The overall goal, it should be remembered, is to increase a child's *wholeness.* The hectic life of the young child is often fractured, as are the equally distracting activities of the older child. What is needed is some type of centered cohesion. Functionally, times of prayer can provide this balance.

We cannot wait until the child quiets down, because we may be waiting for a long time. Prayer can provide its healing function at times of considerable activity or even disaster. There should, of course, be some kind of preliminary calm stage if possible. Also, no approach to prayer should be one which increases a child's franticness, adds to activities or speeds up the tempo. For this reason, the simplest approaches should always be valued.

Although spontaneous experiences can certainly be memorable, there is no substitute for a *regular routine*. The process is not a matter of how many hours a month you can spend in prayer, any more than eating for six hours one day in thirty would satisfy physical needs. A few minutes each day are much more valuable than an hour each week. Set a realistic schedule which can be kept.

Only be with *one child at a time*. On many occasions I have been told by parents how there is no sibling competition in their family and then watched an attempt at prayer utterly deteriorate when the parent was trying to guide two children at once. It is unfair to the children to complicate the issue of prayer in this way. There should, of course, be times of general family prayer, but these should include all of the family members and be conducted as any common religious experience.

Do not be afraid of *discipline*. It is natural that children would have trouble distinguishing this activity from other interpersonal transactions with the same parent. Consequently they might try the same attention-getting mechanisms or engage in the same power struggles they use elsewhere. A stern word is usually all it takes to indicate that this is a different realm. We get upset when we cannot lead a child into holiness by the sheer force of our own personal piety. "Jesus would not be warning a child to shape up," we seem to be saying to ourselves. Well, in fact, there is nothing to suggest that he would not! He was very realistic in relation to people.

At no time in our relations with a child is it more important to remind ourselves that we do not own the child than when we are praying. He or she is *God's child*. Our responsibility is to prepare children for life. That life will be immeasurably richer if it will include a good spiritual foundation. When we are teaching a child we are truly in God's service. That is an awesome responsibility, but one which is at the very essence of our responsibility toward the child, God and ourselves. The years of intense care and concern will be relatively short, and it will not be long before these children will, like the young Jesus, have to be about their Father's business (Lk 12:49).

As a child grows, the parent's particular approach to prayer has to be put into practice and shared. In my own case, I tend toward the imageless side of the prayer scale discussed above. I would like to be in a kind of emotionless state, a sort of Christian Zen, but in reality I rarely approach this. On the emotional to intellectual scale I am much more toward the affective or emotional than the cognitive or mental speculation end. And since I have a natural suspicion of methods, and resist them wherever possible, I tend to fit fairly comfortably into an old monastic prayer, which was a kind of methodless method.

Lectio Divina
In its simplest form, it begins by choosing a scriptural passage. This is not something to be studied but rather approached with awareness of the presence of God. The passage is repeated, memorized, perhaps repeatedly spoken, so that the body and the mind are both involved in the process. Eventually the words begin to drive out everything else. Then we begin to consider what this passage means in our life. This is a sort of openness to conversion or spiritual awareness. This aspect is given the term "meditatio." Fairly shortly thereafter, in a kind of realization of one's relationship to God, there is a response which comes forward. It is probably an affective reaction, such as love or sorrow. This will eventually explode into a prayer ("oratio"). Often there follows a quiet emptiness in which we surrender to God's call and simply rest in his presence ("contemplatio").[5]

The foregoing process is simple to share, even though I am often not at all sure what is transmitted. It can become like yeast in the bread dough of a child's own prayer experience.

Not too long ago I was with a nine-year-old who evidenced interest in prayer. We began by going into a general discussion about parts of the "Jesus Story" that were interesting to her. After talking for a while there seemed to be one particular Gospel story which excited her and with which I could personally resonate. I suggested that we read it. So we went to the chapel and we read it more or less together. I pointed to a short phrase in the reading which seemed to capsulate the essence of the story. We had on previous occasions discussed this particular method of prayer and could move without much explanation. We sat down in the back of the chapel. I suggested that we start repeating the phrase quietly to ourselves over and over, but that we move our lips. The late afternoon sunlight gave a peaceful environment which encouraged us to relax. After a while I began to automatically open up my life to this phrase and suggested that she do the same. My suggestion was, "If Jesus were saying this to us right now, how would it fit into your life?" After a few seconds I felt her hand on mine. I took it and we just sat there quietly for a while. Then I suggested that we say something back to God, that we pray "to" God. I reminded her that we did not have to use any words, that a feeling, like a smile in the heart, was enough. After a little while she slowly took her hand away. I could tell that there was some nervousness. I suggested that she repeat the phrase again and she relaxed. I further suggested that she breathe deeply and slowly and just concentrate on the words of the phrase and her breathing. In a number of non-verbal ways I could guess that she was again at home in the situation. I said something about letting us slow down so that God could catch us. A little bit later I said something else about resting in God. She seemed quite content to just be there. After about five minutes I took her by the hand. We walked forward, and knelt down toward the center of the chapel. I put my arm around her and we just stayed there for a short time. Then we got up and left in the ordinary way. I did not talk to her at all about the experience or indicate to her that she should have felt in any particular way. In fact, as soon as possible we got into some other kind of activity. Soon she was off by herself, following her own rhythm, going to look at some animals. The next Sunday, several days later, I was able to talk to her while on a walk about what happened to her and to me when we were praying in this fashion. I think the discussion encouraged her to attempt the experience on her own.

The foregoing is simply an example of how I tried to translate a personal practice into the prayer life of a young person I found myself in the position of guiding. The specifics are not important. Each adult is going to have to explore to find his or her own way.

12. A Program for Spiritual Growth: Outward Bound

In this chapter are the final four steps of this suggested program. They have a common outward-flowing rhythm and are a natural continuation of what has gone before, not unlike the process of breathing in and breathing out.

These steps are not possible in any sort of meaningful way until a child has experienced "the Other." These are areas of concern at all ages, but are more associated with later childhood than most of the other steps.

Step 9. *Prophecy*

A prophet is a person who is inspired or fired up by God. Prophecy has little to do with foretelling the future. Perhaps the best definition of the Hebrew word for the biblical prophets ("nabi") would be: "One who speaks on behalf of God," or, to shorten it, "God's man" or "God's woman." In this case we are speaking of "God's boy" or "God's girl."

The functional benefit to society of any prophet is to balance the abuses or deficiencies of the institutional person. Most frequently in the famous prophets there has been a conflict between a ruler's personal needs (or the needs of a part of society) and the common good or the worth and dignity of the individual. The prophets have been seen as one of God's means for upholding the common good and individual worth against individuals or nations turning their backs on God's law. Such a theology accepts the common good and individual dignity as essential to the establishment of the reign of God. Let us just look at two famous young prophets.

The great Jeremiah was in his early teens when he heard God's call to be a "prophet to the nations." He protested rather understandably to God, "I do not know how to speak, I am a child!" (1:6). But Yahweh brushed aside this concern: "I am putting my words into your mouth" (1:9). When Jeremiah was born Israel was in a fool's paradise. It was a period of relative prosperity. Most of the people were too occupied with material matters to remember their history or their covenant with God. The good life had become an obsession.

Using the homey image of a pot on the boil, Yahweh told Jeremiah that disaster was about to boil over, despite the placid national scene. Jeremiah tried to wake up a nation that was happy in its slumber, whose priests "have never asked 'Where is Yahweh?'" (2:8). The nation and its priests did not appreciate Jeremiah's interference. Nonetheless, God's child prophet has now become an important part of our spiritual saga.

There is also the magnificent story of Susanna and the youth Daniel. This Jewish tale (in Greek) is appended to the Hebrew text of the Book of Daniel.[1] Here we find an innocent young woman bathing and trapped by two lustful elders of authority in the community. Given a choice of either giving herself to them or being accused of adultery with an imaginary young man, Susanna preferred to remain innocent rather than "sin in the eyes of the Lord" (13:23). The rejected elders swore falsely, but eloquently, to her guilt. They had her unveiled so that even in condemning her they could "feast their eyes on her beauty" (13:32). An outraged community condemned her to death. In her despair she prayed to the Lord.

> The Lord heard her cry and, as she was being led away to die, he roused the holy spirit residing in a young boy named Daniel, who began to shout, "I am innocent of this woman's death!" At which all the people turned to him and asked, "What do you mean by these words?" Standing in the middle of the crowd he replied, "Are you so stupid, sons of Israel, as to condemn a daughter of Israel unheard, and without troubling to find out the truth? Go back to the scene of the

trial: these men have given false evidence against her"
(13:44–49).

Then the young Daniel cleverly proved the elders' lies and hypocrisy. Even against the mighty power of two elders of Israel, God's sense of justice for the innocent was to triumph.

Most would say that situations such as those above are unlikely to arise in the twentieth century family, school, parish or neighborhood. Nonetheless, we must encourage and train our little Jeremiahs and Daniels if we are to be a whole people. It is not enough for a child to be content to learn about God and related matters. Now he or she must participate in our awareness of God and his way, even to teach. It is primarily a matter of attitude.

A not uncommon example of this process is the parent or a teacher who is preparing a disinterested child for a sacrament. If the little Daniel should ask "Why should Joey be confirmed if it does not mean anything to him?" we should listen. Here as institutional adults, we are concerned with the orderliness of a situation, and anyone would consider our attitude reasonable. Yet, if these sacramental gifts are as great as we say they are, why do we drag unwilling children into them? The little Daniel is not just attempting to upset the apple cart. His central query should make us realize that we are about to sacrifice our authenticity. Who is to say that God did not speak through him, at least indirectly? Is this not a gift, a charism?

A central issue for the people of God today is the necessary tension between the good order of the institution and the essential spontaneous grace of the charismatic element. Some theologians, like Hans Küng, seem to find divine authority only in the charismatic. Others, like Church bureaucrats, take the opposite view. Avery Dulles insists that both elements are needed, and he adds:

> The tension between adherence to accepted patterns and adaptation to emerging situations has been felt in the Church since the first generation.[2]

We are our most "institutional" when it comes to children.

This is natural. However, we should recognize this tendency and take care to cultivate the wisdom of our children.

Comparing the simplicity of his disciples to the purity of childhood, Jesus prayed: "I bless you, Father, Lord of heaven and of earth, for hiding these things from the learned and the clever and revealing them to mere children" (Mt 11:25). What spiritual gifts can we hope for from our young prophets? Paul makes the strong point that the gifts of prophecy benefit the whole community, unlike some other gifts. To Paul there seemed to be three principal benefits to the community: improvement, encouragement, and consolation (1 Cor 14:3). These can also be the gifts received by a family or school community.

There is a rather subtle process for the formation of prophets. It cannot be effectively accomplished through any methodology. The child can be encouraged through such questions as "What would Jesus do? Would Jesus be bothered in this situation? Well, since Jesus isn't here and you are, what do you think you could do?" Or radical saints, like Francis, could be referred to in the same way. Contemporary biographies of the saints can be regularly used. Quite a few saints had the courage to listen to something inside of them when things did not seem right. They frequently spoke out, even when they were alone. We have to affirm a child's tendency to speak out in this way, rather than to "respect his/her elders" beyond a constructive point. The main stumbling block here is probably our reluctance to be caught in an inconsistency, or to give up our image of moral superiority. But sooner or later the child is going to find us out anyway. Better it should be while there is still a relationship of great love and trust. So, if we can overcome our own problems, these gifts of prophecy can enrich our communities by encouraging children to share their reactions to various life situations. At the same time we lead children to understand their significance and importance in the community and the awareness that they can be the instrument of the coming of the kingdom of God.

Family Council
A growing number of families or school communities use the family council method for social harmony. Basically it involves

a truly democratic discussion and decision making procedure with each person, adult or child, having an appropriate voice. This concept can be expanded to religious or spiritual concerns. For example, if a problem of discrimination has come up in the neighborhood, we can ask, "What would Jesus do?" The most important part of this process is not to involve the children in a social action program, although that would also be beneficial. This is training to help children realize that we must all share our inspirations if we are to decide what God wants us to do. If in such a discussion we encourage the children to share their views, they will begin to value them.

When we look into the eyes of a child we should remember that these are God's children. What Yahweh said to the prophet Jeremiah could be said about the children whom God has placed temporarily in our care:

> Before I formed you in the womb, I knew you;
> Before you came to birth I consecrated you;
> I have appointed you as a prophet to the nations (Jer 1:5).

Step 10. *Praying for a Vision*

One of the significant moments of spiritual growth in many Native American tribes was when a young member sought an individual perspective for his or her life. This was more than a pattern of thought, or paradigm. It was more like a blueprint for what each individual was to do in constructing the Indian equivalent of the kingdom of heaven.

In the Great Plains, the older boy was sent to a sweat lodge where his body and spirit were cleaned and refreshed. In the aloneness, and without food, he waited for a special dream or vision that would give him his identity in life. Sometimes, as with the great Sioux holy man and Catholic catechist, Black Elk, this vision came at a time of youthful illness. Those who have been around seriously ill youngsters can testify that even today's rather pampered young people usually exhibit amazing maturity and spiritual clarity when in these circumstances.

In some of the northwestern tribes, the young warrior to be was sent out on a trip with very little food. He had to rely upon

God for help. He would travel, in effect, until the Spirit found him. When that occurred he would spontaneously dance. It was a special moment, a benign possession. Then the child/man would return to his family and community and dance his dance before them. If it was verified to be truly a spirit dance he was then recognized as being a contributing spiritual member of the community. At significant moments in his life, including near the time of his death, he would dance this dance to bring strength to himself and to his people. Somewhat similar phenomena can be observed in our present programs of outdoor survival education. One of the most successful programs for juvenile delinquency I have observed was an informal concept of a volunteer worker. She simply would take fairly hard delinquent girls out with her for a two-week period into the desert. The two of them would walk out with only what they had on their backs.

Some Indians on the east coast would take their boys at the beginning of puberty and train them to seek and understand visions and dreams. Through this process a special relationship developed between the child and a guiding spirit helper. In the puberty fast of the Menominee (Great Lakes), the father was the child's guide. The boy would fast. If he had an evil vision he would eat to rid himself of it. So long as he was having good visions he would continue his fast in order that they would be set permanently into his life to the benefit of himself and his dependents. It was not unusual to fast for as long as ten days. The weakened physical condition was balanced by a heightened spiritual activity.

Among the neighboring Winnebagoes the child was to expect a special spiritual gift, such as healing, together with instructions, in the vision, on how to use the gift. These instructions almost always contained ceremonial language and understanding.

Principles

What are some of the common elements in these customs which can provide guidelines for us? We will concentrate on four:

1. A child without a vision was conceived as not being a

whole person. It was not enough to have just the family vision or the vision of his peer group. There was the need for individual visions in order to be whole.

2. The process called forth and demonstrated individual strength, especially going without food, physical discomfort and being deprived of companionship. There was the element of a trial and it was taken seriously. However, it is interesting that there are no stories that I have heard that would indicate that many, if indeed any, ever failed the trial.

3. Even despite the highly individualistic nature of the process, it was always seen as a community affair. The gifts and the viewpoints of the person would be needed to fit into the overall community to make it whole.

4. From the process came an appreciation of the language of ceremony. In Native American cultures what I have termed "religious" in this book (an objective response) tended to follow after the development of a spiritual (subjective) response in the individual's life. A permanent bridge was built between inner and outer expression.

At Confirmation?

In confirming we ask that children "be sealed with the gift of the Holy Spirit." Certainly this relates to "praying for a vision." As theoretically appealing as it might be to make confirmation into this experience, it is practically impossible. From the child's, the parents', and often the clergy's viewpoint, confirmation is a sort of graduation or reward for having simply reached a certain age. Reserving it only for those who wished to really spiritually convert their lives would be at this time unthinkable in many quarters.[3] Besides, a substantial number of parents are not that closely related to denominations which confirm.

A Special Time

Giving up on using existing structures in the Christian sacramental framework to achieve this "praying for a vision" step, we must find a special time where one child and one sensitive adult guide can go off together. There are always reasons to argue against such an arrangement, but it would not take much observation to find that in most families there is a great deal of wasted and even dulling time spent in front of the television or at similar activities. This time could be put together to provide a once-in-a-lifetime two-week camping trip for a parent and child who have prepared themselves to be available for the Spirit.

Ceremony

The one area left to be discussed has to do with ceremony. Children growing up in a Christian environment become very blasé about the rituals of Christian worship. They sometimes look upon all ceremonial language as artificial. Yet there is a spirituality that can be expressed through the dance of ritual which cannot be communicated in words or thoughts. There is a wholeness which comes from letting the inner experience express itself through the body and its movement. One way of accomplishing this is to have the youngster in contact with someone who has a real gift for explaining sacramental language, who appeals not only to the head but to the heart. Such people are rare. But a larger group of people, including many parents, can convey their sense of respect, especially to central themes such as Eucharistic celebrations.

Step 11. *Being the Hands of God*

Some Quakers say of men and women's relation to God, "We are all he has," meaning that we are God's laborers in building the joyful and just kingdom. Whatever God does, he is going to do through us.

Of course, part of the process is to decide how we bear witness to our faith and provide that characteristically Christian concern for service to our brothers and sisters in corporal and spiritual need. But this is a difficult process to hand to the young child. It is better for us to focus on the other part of the procedure, that is, how to carry out the work once we have decided what to do. The child could be seen as an apprentice in the craft of being the hands of God. Rather than finding special service projects for children, I strongly favor making a place for a child in adult projects until at least junior high school age. In other words, it is important for the parent or the foster godparent to teach the child the craft and the proper spiritual attitude.

No amount of classroom discussions about social needs could possibly equal the process in those families in several of our larger cities in which, during a recent hard winter, homes were opened to the homeless just before the Christmas holidays. Equally, there is nothing as meaningful to a young child as to give, not from a surplus or abundance, but in a way that hurts. When a child donates a toy with special meaning to a collection for poor children, rather than one which is about ready to be thrown away, it is an important time for comprehending the mystery of love.

These events happen in the quiet corners of family life. Of course, this means that we as parents or foster godparents have to learn to practice ourselves this concept of service and witness as a spiritual experience.

As children grow they will become sensitive to the hypocrisy in the gap between the words and the actions of the institutional Churches. Many who have failed to see the witness of the comfortable Christian in regard to the poor and unfortunate in our world have turned in disgust from the Church. But fairly often the reverse has also taken place. As Dom Helder Camara remarked in a speech to young people, many of whom had serious doubts about the Christian position:

> Your position with regard to religion and God depends to a great extent on our attitude and our response to life. When you meet people who are trying to live a religion which refuses to be an opium of the masses, an alien and alienating force; when you meet people for whom the love of God involves human love, your atheism will give way to respect, to sympathy—who knows?—to faith.[4]

Getting Organized

Who in the family becomes the foreman for God's crew? Often this is a good position for a parent who feels somewhat uncomfortable with the role of guiding the more subjective practices, but who nonetheless shares the concern for the approach to formation reflected in this program. Where do we start? Of course, there will always be projects needing volunteers. But for the sake of the child's formation, it is better to work in small areas. This is perhaps not the most efficient method of solving immediate human need, but that is not the issue. The best place to begin is probably with the simple admonitions in Matthew (25:35–40) to feed the hungry, give drink to the thirsty, welcome the stranger, clothe the naked, and visit the sick and those in prison. But how do we do this? The lesson we learn from people like the brothers at Taizé and Mother Teresa's Missionaries of Charity is not to give money or food or advice, but to give *ourselves.* What we are called to do is to share our life with the life of those in need, to show our solidarity with the total life of the poor and oppressed.

The person we are helping must remain a person and cannot be made into an object. So often the American way of charity gives to people's physical needs in such a way that we remove from them their sense of dignity. We have to guide our children in approaching those in need as equal brothers and sisters. It is not a Christian act to do something because it will make us feel good, or less guilty.

Once at Christmas time I took a very young boy on a shopping trip. I looked in the store window for a gift. Nearby was a Salvation Army member with the traditional pot and bell. I gave the boy some change and suggested that he might want to put it in the pot, feeling that this might help "teach what Christmas was all about." Just a bit later he came up to me and asked for some more money. I was rather hopeful that this was a sign of developing consciousness and was fairly pleased with myself. However, when I observed the scene I saw quite a different situation. The child would run up and throw a single coin, like a penny or a nickel, into the pot. He would then jump back and watch enthralled as the Salvation Army member unconsciously went through a necessarily automatic ritual—a nod, two double rings and a "Thank you and Merry Christmas." The child was not giving to the poor. He was paying for a performance! This was a definite "I-It" relationship.

The Theological Framework

We should be aware of the concern for social justice in Christian teaching today—specifically that every person has a right to the good life. We all have the obligation not to hoard the gifts that God gives us but to share them in a responsible way. As we take our young sons and daughters out to let their hands do the work of God we are also touching upon some significant theological issues. Moral theologian Bernard Häring presents it this way:

> This is a basic principle of Catholic social doctrine as it has developed since the encyclical *Rerum Novarum* of Leo XIII. The goal is a participatory society and culture in *solidarity* and *subsidiarity*. What the individual can do responsibly should not be taken over by the community, and what the more fundamental communities can achieve by themselves should not be abrogated to the larger organizations. The higher level should supply where the lower one is unable to do so, but principally with the intention to enable and encourage all to fulfill their own functions by creative participation in culture.

> This vision applies also to the problem of *ownership*. The meaning and justification of private property goes only so far as *all* benefit in its purpose, namely, the creative and responsible use of things for one's own person-culture and needs, and for the common good.[5]

We should teach children to approach the people we are helping with unconditional positive regard. This is sometimes hard to do, given the practical circumstances of an individual's life. But we can remember and teach Mother Teresa's concepts that she finds Christ, in a very literal way, in those whom she helps each day.

The First Steps

Charity appropriately begins at home. With very young children there is a spiritual lesson to be learned when they see dad give up, without grumbling, a Saturday afternoon football game on television to go over and fix grandma's clogged gutter. It is important to take the young child along. Tagging along is one of the best ways of beginning an apprenticeship. Holding the ladder or "helping" some way is important. As the child approaches school age, more independent action can be encouraged. There is no end of possibilities. Most parents are in a much better position to suggest ways of demonstrating Christian charity with their own children than someone outside of their family. I would, however, simply recommend one thing that I have found very helpful, which is a modification of a Zen Buddhist practice.

Secret Good Deeds—"Ingi-gyo"

First we must become aware of the needs of others. In the Zen monastery this goes along with the need for increased awareness about everything. It is important for a person to notice, for example, that a monk has put his or her washing on the line and it looks as if it might rain. Perhaps we observe that another has a broken sandal strap.

The next step is to find a time to help out when no one will know we did it. Children love to enter into this practice as a game. Certainly a child is usually lacking the ego detachment of a Zen monk. Children want recognition for their virtue and at other times cannot contain themselves with their "secret." Nonetheless, I have found this to be a good long-range training exercise, if, as with everything else in this book, it is conducted on a regular basis over a period of time.

The foregoing exercise provides an opportunity for interesting discussions about needs. It is an opportunity to gently raise awareness of other people's needs and to provide some guidelines on being able to distinguish between true needs and projecting our own desires. If we ask how a grandfather who nods off in the afternoon can be helped, we may hear from a hungry child that grandfather "wants a candy bar." But without much trouble it can be shown that a true need might be to take the puppy somewhere else to keep it from barking and waking up grandfather.

When the child is slightly older there can be a natural transition to the needs of the larger community. It is not difficult to find an elderly person with a need for a lawn mowed or groceries delivered, or simply to be accompanied when he or she goes to the bank to cash a Social Security check. Once we begin to commit ourselves and to encourage our children to a regular half hour a week or more process of being the hands of God, other opportunities usually automatically suggest themselves.

The children in my life have often been enthusiastic about ignored projects, such as cleaning out the basement at a settlement house, something which the busy staff had always wanted to do but could never find the time. Naturally, as with all children, their hearts explode when they think of children their own age in desperately poor situations, and in recent years they have been especially interested in children cared for by the Missionaries of Charity in various parts of the world. I think that even in these situations, where they will never actually see the faces of the people they are helping, it is important to have some kind of personal contact—to at least have the name of the sister or brother who is working with the children abroad.

If funds are to be collected, then it should be money that the children earn or deprive themselves to obtain. There are a growing number of families who give a joint family gift at Christmas time. It is also nice to have a donation narrowed down to a particular situation, like food for children in a certain place.

There is no end to the possibilities for personal involvement in the tremendous problems we face today. Again, what is suggested here may not be the most effective way of solving a problem, but it is a way of training tomorrow's Christian leaders. The sensitization toward the needs of others will perhaps motivate the next generation to try harder to find the causes for these problems, which are so scandalous in the world's family.

We speak of the corporal works of "mercy." But mercy seems to mean linguistically, and perhaps theologically, giving what the recipient does not deserve. The issue for tomorrow's Christians will be: Are these not really the corporal works of "justice"? Are we giving what the other person has a right to receive? More important, can tomorrow's society, unlike ours, be motivated to find a solution out of love rather than compulsion? The answer may well lie in the early spiritual training of today's children. If they can see a link between this process and their experience of God, there is some hope.

The child sitting on your lap now will have to reach an understanding with a child sitting on another adult's lap at this moment in another part of the world, or in a different socio-economic setting. If they do not, then in twenty years' time they are going to end up hurting or even killing each other over basic issues of life. The solution begins when the children can still take hold of our hands and walk out with us to meet the world in a Christian way.

Step 12. *Learning to Endure*
The last area to be discussed is perhaps the most difficult for caring adults. In raising children we must at times appear heartless in order to reflect our true love. The track coach is not doing a good job unless he or she will force the team to push to the limits of their strength in order to develop new strengths.

In Buddhist literature there is a tale about a spiritual teacher who was instructing a young prince in fencing. They met every day for an hour. One day the prince came to him and explained that the king was ill. The prince knew that he would be required to undertake some duties of state that day. Therefore, he was unable to have his usual daily lesson. But because the prince respected his teacher he came to tell the teacher personally. The teacher instantly grabbed his sword and furiously attacked his student. Desperately the prince defended himself for an exhausting hour. At the conclusion, in amazement and irritation, he asked the teacher to explain why he had proceeded in these circumstances. "Because, my prince," his guide gently explained, "I have few opportunities to teach you that you are not the slave of circumstances."

Among the original North American peoples it was most clearly recognized that endurance and patience were required as virtues if the spiritual life was ever to flower. Discomfort and inconvenience are not always our enemies.

Today's child lives in a push-button age. If it is dark we turn on the electric light. Moods can be as easily corrected with a bottle or a pill. This attitude is reinforced in countless television commercials, and, unfortunately, by the vast majority of adults a child will encounter. We try hard to remove trouble from our children's paths, especially if it represents a type of difficulty that caused us concern when we were young. We do not want them to "suffer" as we did. But in attempting to shield them from these problems in childhood, we may inadvertently be encouraging a weakness that will grow and cause substantial difficulty in adult life. Every day we make many choices concerning our children. It is important that we love them enough to make sure that not all of these choices are responding to a desire for the easy way out. While we are with them is the time to help our children develop the necessary skills to grow into men or women of faith.

Storms accompany all bornings. It is in the wild turbulence that we learn the skills of our growth.

As we, adult or child, travel along our paths, there may be many beautiful springtimes. But without the cold and barren winter there would be no spring beauty. Inconvenience can be a friend, a beacon. It can point out the direction of our pilgrimage. The bud must go through the discomfort of unfolding or it will shrivel. If we use our cleverness to avoid discomfort we will miss valuable lessons. Bodily discomfort tells us when we have broken nature's rhythm. The pain in the heart can also draw us back to a more harmonious life and prepare us for a new step.

Life is like a ladder. We climb up a rung, and then when we regain our composure, we may become very comfortable on that rung. Perhaps we even become an expert on the rung. We do not want to become a struggling beginner again. Yet, if we learn that each step is only a rung, we will welcome the freshness of each new beginning. And each step we take in life becomes an act of renewal.[6]

13. Dreams and Journals

Chapters 9–12 have presented a suggested specific program for spiritual formation. Before closing this practical section we should also examine a more natural program which is available to all and is already a part of each person's makeup.

Self-Exploration

The "real" world has an interior dimension which we as adults frequently ignore or even deny. As a result, when we do individually discover some evidence of an interior reality we generally over-react. We set up a false dichotomy between inner and outer experience. We also tend to see inner world activities as some kind of a ladder leading to the development of a higher consciousness. We can become so lost in our inner world that we never fully reappear.

As has been stated above, the "inner world" is only a metaphor. What we are experiencing is simply part of our total present response to life. It is an unusual phenomenon simply because we have been denying its existence for some time. Certainly, whatever is coming from our interior existence is a part of our here and now experience and is not a voyage to some spiritual Olympus.

In young children the interior and exterior dimensions are more in balance. This fact itself can occasionally cause trouble. To a very young child there may be no difference between the nightmare and the actual world. But otherwise this unified approach is generally beneficial. It means that a child can take

quite naturally things which are experienced in the interior dimension, whereas adults tend to make much of the same thing.

A few words of caution are in order. The purpose of exploring the interior dimension as it is presented here is *not* to analyze but to *hear.* There is a rich experience around us and inside
of us. In fact we *are* a rich experience. It is enough to become
aware of this experience. To ask "why" is to set ourselves an
impossible task. We will be frustrated in two ways: there is no
full answer, and in attempting to find an answer we stop the dynamic process of listening to our own experience. If there must
be a question it should be not "why" but "what."

With stable and secure children there is little danger of the
kind of preoccupation we see among people who are fascinated
by the self-exploration process. There is, however, some danger
that a parent can become overly impressed and communicate to
the child that more should be made of the experience than is in
fact productive. Today we talk about self-investment, self-
awareness, self-improvement. The age-old problem of preoccupation with self is a danger in these quests. It is as if we have
hypnotized ourselves while looking in a mirror and focus only
on our own image. We refuse to move, wanting more knowledge, more spirituality, more self. We become very conscious of
the self. We become stuck. This demand for more self goes in
circles and is not really self-exploration. Thomas Merton describes the process of turning self-awareness into preoccupation
with self:

> This brings with it an instinct to study themselves, to shape
> their lives, to remodel themselves, to tune and retune all
> their inner dispositions—and this results in full-time medita-
> tion and contemplation on *themselves.* They may unfortu-
> nately find this so delightful and absorbing that they lose all
> interest in the invisible and unpredictable action of grace. In
> a word, they seek to build their own security, to avoid the
> *risk* and *dread* implied by submission to the unknown mys-
> tery of God's will.[1]

Should you become concerned about things your child is
sharing with you, or if the child becomes disturbed by particular

experiences, you should consult with an appropriate professional, if for no other reason than simply to be reassured.

Dreams

Before the advent of modern psychology the dream was frequently seen as a process by which God would deliver his messages. In Genesis (28:10–22) we learn of the great dream of Jacob's ladder. It was so powerful that Jacob named the place where he dreamed "Beth-El," that is, "The House of God." "Jacob awoke from his sleep and said, 'Truly, Yahweh is in this place and I never knew it! ' " (v. 16). This is a good way of looking at a dream. Often when we are dreaming we are in "The House of God" and we do not realize it.

There are many other practical uses of dreams in the Bible. Matthew tells us that God explained Mary's pregnancy to Joseph in a dream, and "when Joseph woke up he did what the angel of the Lord had told him to do" (Mt 1:24). Scripture also warns us that making too much out of dreams or applying our own cleverness to them can be dangerous. The Old Testament law of holiness (Lev 17—26) probably condemns the interpretation of dreams. Ecclesiasticus reminds us that "dreams put fools in a flutter" (34:1) and that "divination, auguries and dreams are nonsense" (34:5).

Morton Kelsey has documented the history and relationship of dreams in Judaeo-Christian religious experience.[2] Through a Christian interpretation of Carl Jung's theories, Kelsey has done much to help contemporary Christians reclaim an important part of their spiritual heritage, and has helped to balance the various fads which have developed in secular circles over the past two hundred years.

Dream Theory

There was a tendency in psychology before Sigmund Freud to believe that the dream was simply a random opening of memory banks. In time Freud may be primarily remembered for his strong argument that a dream is not a chance happening. Through this we were able to return to the dream as a form of communication, a dialogue. Unfortunately, Freud's specific dream theories were quite narrow and pushed to ridiculous extremes by some of his followers. He saw the dream as a time for wish fulfillment and the acting out of frustrations. Furthermore, he saw most frustrations as sexual, and the symbols of dreams were examined primarily for their sexual meaning. This gave rise to popular "Dream Dictionaries" and all manner of curious follies. Unfortunately, in the political struggles within psychology Freudian concepts were given much predominance.

To the practical Alfred Adler a dream focused on an individual's present problems and was often a way of preparing for the next day. In addition he felt that the dream always contained an expression of a person's "lifestyle," that is, our individual processes for unifying our experience and organizing our approach to life's problems and possibilities.

Jungian and Gestalt psychology provide especially helpful approaches for people who wish to use their dreams as tools for self-exploration. According to Jung, dreams frequently point the way in which we could grow and develop. Through the dreams voices deep within us are brought to the surface. Our unconscious tells a story to the conscious self. Unencumbered by all the details that preoccupy the conscious self, the unconscious can get a clearer view of the situation and even predict the outcome of a course of action. To Jung there were no universal meanings to symbols. Each person develops his or her own unique language for communication between the unconscious and the conscious self. The story of the dream is basically a creative act and is to be approached as we would view a painting. "Let the dream speak" is Jung's recurring advice.

The dream, in Jung's theories, is also a part of the complex balancing process of human self-regulation. If in our conscious lives we are out of balance, then, according to Jung's compensatory principle, a balance will be supplied by the unconscious. For example, a daytime life of thinking without awareness of feelings might be balanced by dreams full of raw emotions.

Dreams, according to Jung, frequently express basic issues that go beyond a person's specific concerns. We can take clay and make a statue. The statue is unique and different from any other statue, but it also remains clay. From time to time my dreams may convey a message from my clay, that part of me that is common to all people.

Jung makes a very valuable distinction between symbols and signs. A sign is less than what it represents. A road sign pointing in the direction of a city is certainly less than the city. A symbol stands for something more than is obvious. A great dragon breathing fire can be a symbol of my anger. A sign is always linked to the conscious thought behind it, whereas symbols are more natural and spontaneous events. In other words, no one ever invented a symbol.[3]

Gestalt psychology considers a person as a total organism, with formed patterns. A person's dreams are integrated with these patterns and are an important tool for becoming more truly aware of the total organism. Fritz Perls taught that every part of my dream is me. I have created the dream, therefore, I am each part. If I dream of myself and an aggressive friend, I have chosen my friend as a symbol of that aggressive part of me. I can, therefore, play or "speak for" each part, person, and object in the dream. My personification of the part helps me hear the dream. The object is not to interpret or analyze, but to become aware of the dream and as a result to become aware of me.[4]

Since the 1950's we have been aware that when people dream their eyes move rapidly. This is called REM, or rapid eye movement, and enables us to learn about dream frequency. Some researchers like to speak of stages of sleep. Two are rather hypnotic or borderline states between waking and going to sleep (hypnogogic), and between sleeping and waking up (hypnopompic), as distinct from the deep period of sleep in between which can in turn be subdivided. Using this framework we can conservatively say that on an average night a person has dreamed at least four times and that each dream would have lasted between ten minutes and an hour. As the night wears on the dreams usually become longer, and the longest dream is frequently just prior to waking. This morning dream has been interpreted in many societies as a preparation dream which might even contain revelations of the future.

There is some evidence for an alternative theoretical framework which suggests inner activity during the entire sleep time.

Perhaps at some point in the future we will discover that we dream continually, even when we are not sleeping. What we are really discussing as "dreams" is our awareness of the dream state. We do know that dreams are necessary for a wholesome life and that interference with the dream process (through drugs, alcohol, etc.) can result in severe emotional disturbance.

It is probably safe to say that an average mature adult dreams about twenty percent of the sleeping time. But a child's dreaming is a different situation. The prematurely born infant dreams eighty percent of sleep time. A child born after the full term of pregnancy dreams fifty percent of sleep time for the first few weeks of life. And since young infants spend so much time asleep, they are in the dream state as much as they are in the non-dream state.[5]

Listening to Dreams

The basic suggestion here is that children be regularly encouraged to express their dreams as a way of recognizing the presence of a non-visible world and as a better way of hearing themselves, and thereby developing more wholeness in their lives. It is not suggested that the dreams be used to help a child "understand" and analyze his or her inner composition, nor that they become an instrument for an adult to influence the child's behavior in *any* way.

Dream sharing is a story-telling time. For a practical demonstration we are indebted to the work of Kilton Stewart who has studied the remarkable role of dreams in the Senoi tribe on the Malay Peninsula. Dreams are discussed every day at breakfast. From early childhood a person is encouraged to master the negative forces presented in the dreams and to act out and implement the positive forces.

> If he dreams of a new trap, the elders help him to construct it to see if it will work. If he dreams a song or poem, the elders encourage him to express it for criticism or approval. If he dreams of a girl, he is encouraged to consummate love with her in his dreams and to court her while he is awake.[6]

Through an awareness of his dreams the Senoi youth travels the road to maturity. Children are given instructions on what to do in future dreams. Stewart's study shows that the children's dreams change in the direction suggested by their elders.

Dreams are not only a tool of personal growth, but play an important role in the development of the Senoi society. The culture accepts whatever is expressed in the dream. This amounts to a full acceptance of the individual. The need for this acceptance cannot be emphasized enough in relation to children. If we as adults accept children's dreams, we accept children as they are. In other words, we do not reject them because they are not what we think they ought to be. The Senoi came to be known as a society completely free of violent crime or mental illness. Working with dreams has been suggested as a way of preventing these and other social evils.

It is not recommended that the Senoi method be followed as a primary means of instruction, but sharing of dreams' stories at breakfast is a routine way of both accepting the children and in turn helping them be more confident in accepting their own inner experiences. The realization that the definition of "me" includes things not visible leads to a sense of wholeness and an openness to spiritual growth.

The following are comments from some children who have routinely shared their dreams in the same family situation over the past several years:

> I feel glad when I share things. I sometimes tell dreams like stories just for the fun of it. . . .I like to tell my dreams because it is nice to share and because it makes me feel good. Sometimes I hate to say my dreams because it makes me cry, usually because it is embarrassing or sad. But if I don't tell my dreams sometimes I become very nervous. . . .When I share my dreams I feel happier, lighter, relieved and not alone. . . . It's nice for people to listen to you even when the dream is sad or weird.

Dream sharing can become a productive method of growth in many dimensions. What is being suggested here is that it is an important adjunct to spiritual growth. It is sufficient simply to have a "dream telling time" in the morning as one might have an evening story telling time or a "what happened to you to-day?" time around the dinner table or the fireside. The less made of the situation the better. Inevitably children who cannot remember a dream and want their share of attention will make one up. If they become too elaborate they should be gently discouraged, perhaps asked to shorten the narrative. But even something made up comes from inner experience and is not lacking in merit.

The Journal

This is the age of journals. We have a number of elaborate forms of journal keeping. It should be remembered, however, that the keeping of journals as a method of dialoguing with ourselves is quite ancient. Some of the most meaningful journals are simple. This is certainly true of the journals of Henry David Thoreau and his beautiful explanations of the simple observations of life around a New England pond.

What is suggested here is not a psychological journal for children, although some take to the experience readily. Rather, it is recommended that the parent keep a journal of the child's spiritual growth, a simple story of each child.

A Spiritual History

The journal might well begin before the child is born. Say something about the world in which the child is being born, as well as the family and its cultural roots.

Use the check list for the twelve step program in Chapters 9–12 every six months to reflect on changes taking place in your child's life. Discuss this with the child. As children grow up they can take an active part in these reflections, and eventually can even help to write them down. The net result is somewhat like a ship's log charting a course through life. It will be of extreme value to them when they are grown. It is well to have a copy made for security and your own memory-time.

Nothing elaborate is being suggested. The parent should feel natural with the process. There is nothing wrong with adding a general story of a person's growth and development, or making it humorous, clever or pictorial. The end result is that there is some kind of a collected story which children can put their hands on and occasionally read. It is available to them as they are able to understand it.

Do not go into extremely specific details. Do not write about things which just happened. Historians need a little time to gain perspective.

It is good to connect a history with events: Christmas, Easter or birthday times. This is a similar process to measuring a child's height on the wall each year. It is surprising how significant any growth processes are to children even in adolescence.

The journal should not stop at the pre-adolescent period but should continue into adolescence, with the child taking more and more responsibility for it.

Feeling and Growth

Good feelings do not necessarily coincide with spiritual growth. The development of the affective side of a child's being is extremely important, but it is not identical to the child's spiritual development. If we look only to those things which made the child laugh, giggle and smile it will be a thin dream-telling time or journal entry. It is unfortunately the case that many people, when suggesting devotional and meditative practices for children, are basically recommending only those things which are entertaining or emotionally stimulating. The spiritual realm is not the place to be primarily focused on those issues. Of course, as a practical matter children are not going to stay with something which is painful or excessively dull, but they are more tolerant than we often suspect. Much in life can be rewarding without resulting in an emotional catharsis.

Focusing too much on the feeling side of a spiritual experience can mean that we are just nibbling when we have been given the opportunity to taste deeply of our spiritual nature.

Part IV
NEW PATTERNS IN CHRISTIAN LIVING

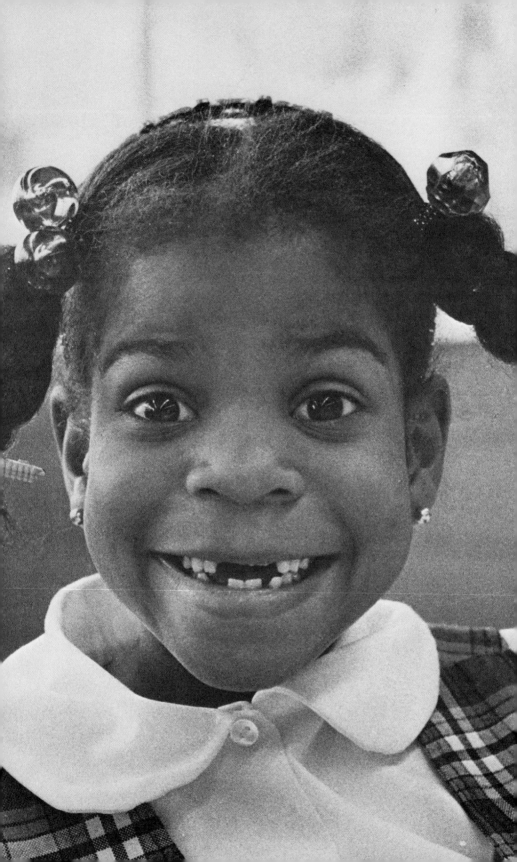

14. Spirituality in the Future

Thinking back to the world as it was constituted when we were ten years old and comparing it to the present can help us appreciate the rapidly accelerating rate of change. Could any of our parents have anticipated the world in which we are living our adult Christian lives?

Karl Rahner and the Future Church

To be of assistance to our children we must realize that they will have to live in circumstances far different than the ones in which they are now being raised. But how can we know what is to come? Most attempts to define the future are merely subjective hopes or fears. Occasionally, however, there is an objective and reasoned stab into the unknown which is of practical help. Such a framework has recently been provided by Karl Rahner, one of the most significant theologians of our age. Born in 1904, Rahner can fully appreciate the problem of change. An influential force at the Second Vatican Council he demonstrated the dramatic mystery of God's relationship with the pilgrim people of God. In his theology Rahner has never underestimated the importance of a spiritual foundation for all other aspects of Christian life and thought. At the same time he warns that spirituality is not an independent force. It develops in relation to the evolution and self-understanding of the Christian community.

Rahner has become known as one who sees the Church of the future as existing in a "diaspora" situation, that is, as a minority in every part of the world and at every level of society. The image refers to the Jewish dispersion after the exile when the people were scattered around the world to live among those who did not share their faith. Rather than developing into an ever-dwindling ghetto cult, Rahner sees us leaping forth as a truly new Church—a *world* Church. We will no longer take a model of Christian life developed in Europe and try to make it fit all situations.

According to Rahner, we are just on the threshold of a radically new chapter in our story as the people of God. There have been two preceding chapters: (1) for a short time we were Judaeo-Christian; (2) then, starting even in the apostolic era, we identified the Church with particular cultural groups—Greek, medieval European, and, finally, modern European. Now, beginning more or less around the time of Vatican II, (3) we see the beginning of a Church whose "living space is from the very outset the whole world."

> Vatican II derives its importance from the fact that it proclaimed—even though only in a rudimentary and vague sort of fashion—a transition from the Western Church to the world Church similar in character to the transition which occurred for the first and only time when the Church ceased to be the Church of the Jews and became the Church of the Gentiles.[1]

Tomorrow's Spirituality

If this be so, then we who have been born at the end of a major period of history are, at this moment, preparing Christians who will be among the first to live in, and perhaps even help to launch, a new era. Like Moses we can but lead the children through the wilderness. We will not fully experience the transition. At least Moses got a glimpse of the promised land. Have we no such helpful perspective?

In a recent work, *Concern for the Church,* Rahner includes a short but vitally important essay on "The Spirituality of the Church of the Future."[2] His concepts have many practical implications for those attempting to guide their children. He presents five factors which may well be characteristic of Catholic spirituality in the future. These have application to other Christian communities as well.

1. Future spirituality will be a continuation of "the old spirituality." It will not "degenerate into a mere humanism of a horizontal type" but will remain "a spirituality of adoration." We must "preserve the memory of the past history of piety" and reject the view that our "piety is continually making a fresh start." Spirituality will not be independent of the Christian community, and it will be "a spirituality of the Sermon on the Mount and of the evangelical councils, continually involved in renewing its protest against the idols of wealth, pleasure and power."[3]

COMMENT: What this should caution us against is searching for the newest fad in spiritual experience. More than we, our children will need to graft their experience onto the history of our people's encounters with God.

The experience in this country in the past two decades of spiritual experimentation outside the Church justifies Rahner's concern. Despite much that was exciting and personally beneficial, few people have developed their spirituality in relation to the reality of their daily lives. For many it has been an escape from that reality and thereby an unsuccessful attempt to stand outside of their own history. It was, and continues to be, a basically horizontal motion of hopping from one refreshing pond to the next. There are, of course, exceptions to this picture, but it is not an unfair description of the total phenomenon.

Today the same thing is happening inside Church circles. Facilitators of spiritual experience often proceed without a "memory of the past history of piety."

But this concern is only a part of the picture. If we are to have a continuation of the "old spirituality" there must be another understanding which leads us to Rahner's second point.

2. The spirituality of the future must be concerned only with "what is most essential to Christian piety." In other words, we are to experience a continuation of the *essential* part of the old spirituality and not all the romantic trappings.

We shall speak of Jesus and not of the Infant of Prague. We shall speak of Mary but have less to do with Lourdes and Fatima.[4]

What then is that core? This is a difficult question which has no clear answer. Rahner gives a theologian's response:

> That God is, that we can speak to him, that his ineffable incomprehensibility is itself the very heart of our existence and consequently of our spirituality; that we can live and die with Jesus and properly with him alone in an ultimate freedom from all powers and authorities; that his incomprehensible cross is set up above our life and that this scandal reveals the true, liberating and beatifying significance of our life.[5]

COMMENT: Does anyone have trouble thinking back to practices which really bordered on superstition or idolatry? We continue dubious practices for children which we ourselves have discarded. Having little Debbie kneel in front of the crèche while we take a photograph can be quite confusing to her. She is trying to figure out if that little doll in the straw is the "real" Jesus. If not, then why is she kneeling, and, if so, then why are not *you* kneeling?

There are many borderline situations which parents must resolve for themselves. For example, what is the rosary? Is it an essential part of our history to which the child should be exposed? Do we use it ourselves? Can it have a modern justification as a good mantra designed to empty out our busyness? Is the practice intellectually absurd? Is it a commendable act of simplicity?

The issue is not so much to draw up a list of "approved" practices but to critically examine all of our devotional practices to see how they relate to the core of Christian spirituality. In this transition era each of us and each community from the family upward in size must quest for at least a tentative sense of the essentials of Christian spirituality.

3. "The Christian of the future will be a mystic or he will not exist at all." This remarkable statement comes from Rahner's belief that already the sociological support systems for Christianity no longer exist. Christians do not find themselves in the Church because of family, society or cultural environment. There is *no* Christian milieu. "Christian faith today (and consequently spirituality) must be continually freshly realized."

For, according to Scripture and the Church's teaching, rightly understood, the ultimate conviction and decision of faith comes in the last resort, not from a pedagogic indoctrination from outside, supported by public opinion in secular society or in the Church, nor from a merely rational argumentation of fundamental theology, but from the experience of God, of his Spirit, of his freedom, bursting out of the very heart of human existence and able to be really experienced there, even though this experience cannot be wholly a matter for reflection or be verbally objectified.[6]

COMMENT: This awareness of the present, and certainly future, social situation has great significance in what we teach our children. Faith *must* be internalized; personal responsibility *must* be emphasized; spiritual growth *must* point directly toward the experience of God. The children we take in our arms must be trained to stand alone. At times they will have nothing but the awareness of God to help them. And at other times they must stand even without that awareness. Conscious choices will have to be made all along the line. Nothing will be taken for granted.

This need to stand alone is coupled with a need to join in community, not as dependents but as strong independent pilgrims.

4. Community is "a real and essential element of the spirituality of tomorrow." First we must admit that at least the Catholic Church of the pre-Vatican II era was essentially a Church of "spiritual individualists" with a "communal liturgy."

Even parishes will become more community oriented if they are to survive:

Parishes in the traditional sense will themselves have to become living community parishes more clearly than hitherto and can no longer remain (more or less) institutions by which the official Church provides for the individual religious needs of isolated individuals.[7]

But "community" can also mean any other person outside myself.

In the spirituality of the future can there not be a kind of guru, a spiritual father giving to another person an instruction filled with the Spirit, which cannot be completely broken down into psychology, theoretical, dogmatic and moral theology?[8]

COMMENT: I find most painful the attempt to make common cause with those Christians who are "coming to church" to be serviced. They were trained to look, often with guilt, to Mother Church to care for them from the cradle to the grave. They grew up in a Church where you prayed alone, sinned alone, confessed alone and died alone. This is the concept of Church which is dying. These Christians are the basically sad people who enter the Christian assembly with blinders. They are here only to relate to the cleric in charge and perhaps through him to God. Despite Vatican II, we have not sufficiently re-examined the countless ways by which the leadership of the Church, clerical, religious *and* lay, perpetuate this depressing state of affairs.

The problems raised by the former age of "isolated individuals" for the spiritual training of today's children are serious. The solutions are not simple. Of course we should avoid privatistic attitudes or a false belief in individual revelations. Spirituality cannot become a private escape from life. A visit to the Blessed Sacrament is pure fantasy if it is in lieu of healing interpersonal relations.

These are some of the negatives and they will be difficult enough, but what about a child's positive preparation for a community-based spirituality?

When we think of the large ecclesial community, a parish of several hundred, or even a small "base" community, there is little way for any special introduction of the child to an especially spiritual perspective. This process has to be delayed to the agenda for the adolescent and young adult.

But the young child can be trained to be open, sharing and authentic about spiritual experience. The process will naturally begin with the parent. In time, Rahner's "guru" will be other adults and finally peers. Community can be just one other person. Neither the difficulties nor the importance of this process should be minimized.

5. Rahner's final point calls for a "new ecclesial aspect" and it parallels his first point of not abandoning our spiritual roots. Perhaps this is more of a hope than a prediction. But, at the least, he invites us to see ourselves as "Church," even though, as he says,

> We feel burdened in the Church both by the reactionary callousness of the institutional factor and by the reckless modernism that threatens to squander the sacred heritage of faith and to destroy the memory of its historical experience. The Church can be an oppressive burden for the individual's spirituality by doctrinalism, legalism and ritualism, to which true spirituality, if it really is authentic and genuine, can have no positive relationship.[9]

But, he says, in effect, just transcend all that; do not let it get you down. In a remarkable pastoral gesture, Rahner speaks to those who have been bruised in various Church conflicts (and who has not?). We all know that "the Church" is not a sign lifted up among the heathens as acclaimed in Vatican I. We know that the Church

> is the poor Church of sinners, the tent of the pilgrim people of God, pitched in the desert and shaken by all the storms of history.[10]

Now, what if we run up against someone who refuses to accept this turn of events? Do not be discouraged, we are counseled. Just assume a

> superior, *duplicate naiveté,* marked by wisdom and patience, which . . . endures as a matter of course the misery and inadequacy of the Church [italics added].[11]

COMMENT: Rahner is asking us to "hang in there," and, when we run across someone with a naive attitude, not to get mad and leave. Stay and duplicate their naiveté on the other side. I do not know how theologians react to that kind of reasoning, but it goes down very well with a spiritual director.

What does this mean for our children? Train them that they are part of the Church, no matter *what* happens in their future life. It is like their home, and, like home, a place they cannot be kicked out of.

Train them that sometimes we have to wait for people to catch up. Sometimes we have to sprint along. Sometimes someone hurts us. Sometimes we hurt someone—but we can never be rejected. We inherently belong to the Christian community. This is *our* Church. These are attitudes which our children will learn more from our actions than our words.

A Joyful Christian Style

If we accept Rahner's outlook, then a characteristic of the spirituality of the future must be a greater vitality than exists at present. The ever fresh spirit of God is not calling our children to be just more bodies at the wake of dead religious institutions. This is a time of budding, not of decay.

Another of today's Christian prophets, Joseph Gelineau, has quested as musician and liturgist for a characteristic Christian style. Gelineau finds this style springing from the Old Testament and flowing into the best moments of our Christian history.

> An expression impregnated by the Spirit of Freedom and love; a body through which the light and love of the risen Christ already shines; a people already saved in hope, who can follow the Lamb wherever he goes.[12]

St. Teresa danced with her sisters; David leaped and sang before the ark of the Lord. Let us at least help tomorrow's Christians prize and exhibit their spiritual joy. We all need it.

15. Faith, Courage, Doubt— and Grace

The first three words in the title of this chapter come from a Buddhist proverb. We are told that there are three things needed for the spiritual pilgrimage, "great faith, great courage, and great doubt."

The lives of our Christian people are filled with examples of courage. Over and over individuals have played the fool to a skeptical world, taken the absurd road, stood up against great odds, and moved hardened hearts through courageous deeds. Non-Christian religious writers have frequently pointed to the faith of Christians as a characteristic of Christianity. And yet that faith is surprisingly fresh and new in each age. "Faith" and "courage" are characteristic virtues of Christianity.

Holy Doubt

"Doubt" however, is another matter. "Great doubt" is almost unknown as a Christian virtue. Yet it is an essential part of the spiritual journey. Once I was trying to justify this position while giving a conference at a contemplative monastery. A young novice was attacking the position. One of the older monks offered to help me out. He surprised everyone by jumping into the middle of the circle. Many years before he had been a boxer, and it seemed for all the world as if he were jumping into the ring. He said:

> Sometimes God says to me, "Go on out there, David," and I say, "Lord, I am frightened. I would rather not." And God

161

says, "Oh, now, get out there, David," so I say, "All right,
Lord," and I jump out to something new. I dive off the end
of the pier; I get right in there into unknown territory. Then
after a while as I am beginning to make it I say, "Hey, Lord, I
did it!" There is no answer. I turn around and God is not
there anymore! And then I say, "God, where are you? You
got me out here; now you've got to help me." But God is
not there. And he does this because he loves me.

Dear Brother David taught us all that afternoon to understand in a unique way the deep truth of the Christian mystics.
"Sometimes," said Meister Eckhart, "for God's sake we must
take leave of God."

If we are to truly know what is of God and what is of our
own making and fantasy we must, at important times of growth,
be without the consolation and comfort of a sure and certain
faith. We grow in the tension between certainty and uncertainty,
between faith and doubt. The Episcopal religious educator John
Westerhoff has suggested that this should be seen as a natural
period, at least in adolescence.

For example, my teenagers sometimes think I am quite stu-
pid and misguided. And while that is not easy to live with, it
is important for them to believe it in order to acquire their
own identity. The same is true of faith. In order to move
from an understanding of faith that belongs to the community to an understanding of faith that is our own, we need to
doubt and question that faith. At this point the "religion of
the head" becomes equally important with the "religion of
the heart," and acts of the intellect, critical judgment, and
inquiry into the meanings and purposes of the story and the
ways by which the community of faith lives are essential.[1]

Westerhoff terms this a period of "searching faith," and it must
be affirmed. He suggests this period should be characterized by:
(1) experimentation where we explore alternatives to our earlier
understanding, and (2) learning to practice "the need to commit
our lives to persons and causes" even when these persons and
causes appear fickle and unwise to the mature world.

In order to continue the Christian tradition at its best, today's searching adolescents will require not only Westerhoff's supportive environment but will need to have already had a strong spiritual life preceding adolescence. They are not simply in a vestibule awaiting real life as a young adult.

Our children will, of course, need to be sustained when they reach their adolescence. They may well become praying atheists. Basically these young men and women will find an opportunity for divine encounter, albeit unusual, even in their crises of faith. They will in fact be able to sanctify their doubt and raise it to a sacramental level. Their strength to do this must come from the spiritual foundation of their early years. Their spiritual life began as infants, with the very moment of birth.

Tomorrow's World Church

At least some of these holy doubters will eventually become the great witnesses to Christianity in the future. They will pass many stages. Some of them will go through a stage of being able to say, "Even if Jesus were not God I would follow him." "Even if Jesus did not rise from the dead I would follow him." And, perhaps, even, "Even if there is no God I will follow him." This is the greatest act of faith—faith without belief. We have a desperate need for this in the complex world we face.

As Anglican Bishop John A. T. Robinson speculates about tomorrow's leaders in the Church:

> . . . they are likely, I would guess, to come in future less from the old centres than the new edges—like liberation theology, black theology, and women's theology. They will be heard too across the frontiers of other disciplines, other ideologies and other faiths. They will come not simply from above nor simply from below. They will arise out of that engagement to holy worldliness, where those like monks and mystics who, in Bonhoeffer's distinction, live life from the inside out meet in creative encounter with that greater number of Christians who will always live it from the outside in.[2]

In the upcoming third millennium of its history, Christianity must truly enter the world. It moves from a people in the last stages of a European Christendom to a truly world religion.[3] That should include not only the third world but also the full extent of the first world, including its alternative subcultures. Like Brother David, Christianity must jump out from time to time even where it cannot find God.

Our young people, out of their personal experiences, can provide guidance for the future Church. The little girl and the little boy whom you are guiding to find an authentic encounter with God today will likely become the doubting Thomas and the doubting Sarah of tomorrow. But the process does not end there. Because of what you are facilitating at this moment of their lives, they will go on to sanctify their doubts and to carry the good news to the world in a unique way.

Our Moment in History

Like the grand inquisitor in Dostoyevsky's *The Brothers Karamazov,* we too can look at Christ and say, "You have no right to add anything to what you have said of old." The old cardinal, even knowing that it was truly Jesus who walked the streets doing good, could have him arrested and prepared to burn at the stake. Jesus was threatening security in his renewed invitation to freedom. Who does not hear youth's impatient call to make this world closer to the kingdom of God by improving the quality of life? And who at times has not been tempted to say to our young people, as did the old cardinal to Christ, "Why, then, have you come to hinder us?" Although we see God in them, we will guard our security and mistrust their quest for freedom.

The ultimate stakes are not simply to help a child find individual salvation or to maintain the future of an institutional Christianity. At issue is the future quality of life for the world itself. The historian Arnold Toynbee has made a simple but profound statement of our moment in history. What follows was published in the late 1960's. Now it appears even clearer:

> The dry places through which emancipated Western Man and his emancipated non-Western disciples now walked, seeking rest, were the spiritual vacuum that they had created

in their own soul, and they were bound to find no rest in this state, considering that it is a state which is contrary to human nature. Their house was empty. It had been swept by rationalism and it had been garnished by science—garnished superbly, but not made hospitable for human habitation, for it still remained empty of religion, and to offer Man science as a substitute for religion is as unsatisfactory as it is to offer a stone to a child who is asking for bread. Modern Western Man and his non-Western fellow-travellers had perforce to replace their ancestral religions by some authentic other religion; and the authentic religions with which they did fill the spiritual vacuum in their souls were certainly more wicked than Christianity had ever been even in those passages of its history in which the temperature of its fanaticism had reached and passed boiling-point. The parable speaks of seven other more wicked spirits. In real life in my generation I can identify three, namely Nationalism, Individualism, and Communism. The enormities that have been perpetrated in the name of each of these three post-Christian ideologies have been, if possible, still more wicked than the worst that have ever been perpetrated in the name of Christianity. Modern Man's state in the age of agony and atrocity that dawned in 1914 has been even worse than modern Western Man's state was in the age of the Catholic-Protestant wars of religion.

Happily, however, this worse state has now turned out not to be the last. The historic higher religions have inaugurated a new chapter in the history of religion by re-emerging unexpectedly, and this in a new mood that presents an encouraging contrast to their traditional mood of mutual envy, hatred, and uncharitableness. The resurgence of the historic religions began, in the interlude between the two world wars, when some of the Protestant Christian churches started the Ecumenical Movement and led some of the Eastern Orthodox Churches to join in. This rejuvenescence of Christianity was given a potent fresh impetus when Pope John XXIII was elected to sit in Saint Peter's chair and when, during his brief tenure of it, he began the *aggiornamento* (the "bringing up to date") of the Roman Catholic Church and carried this movement, before his untimely death, beyond "the point of no return."[4]

Even though we are experiencing some post-Vatican II backlash with a resulting attempt to ignore that we have passed beyond "the point of no return," the fact is that the way back is blocked.

We should not ignore the historical dialectic which has brought us to the position we occupy in the 1980's. The 1950's saw a Church increasingly irrelevant to the world. It spawned a legalistic way of thinking that produced more guilt than healing. The Church was seen as a perfect society, and if you wanted to be saved you were to be good laymen and laywomen and "pray, pay, and obey."

The beginning of the swing away from this static state was felt during the 1960's with Vatican II (1962–1965). Basically the Church was encouraged to address itself to the deep spiritual needs reflected in Toynbee's statement quoted above. We were at last moving to fill the empty house of our times. But this revolutionary moment was not communicated effectively. Many students in one of the largest Catholic universities in the late 1960's heard nothing in their four years about the revolutionary concepts of Vatican II. Because the news is still getting out we cannot say that we are beginning to experience a synthesis between the 1950 Church and Vatican II. The reaction to the old Church is just beginning. The perspective will broaden until we can see the medieval Church as the thesis and the post-Vatican II Church as the antithesis. Then we can begin a synthesis which will probably resemble in some ways the early Church. For the foreseeable future the following issues will be important:

1. We are a pilgrim people constantly in need of reform and revitalization.

2. Christendom is dead. There is no more dream of a "Christian state." The people of God are better imagined as a resistance movement.[5] We are resisting the dehumanization of people. Like the underground in World War II, we are not the whole story of liberation, but an important part of it.

3. Somehow Jesus Christ is central to being a Christian. What does that mean to us? Christ lived and died, but his mo-

ment in time was remarkably prolonged. In fact it is still going on. We are called in the ongoing Christ event to participate in the fundamental sacrament where God's love encounters human existence. We are also called to be disciples in a community of disciples, whose destiny is to make Christ's agenda their own.

The future of Christianity will not be set by the institutional Church but will be formed by the total world community. This bedrock reality has been expressed by Avery Dulles:

> The great decisions affecting man's future are being made in the sphere of the secular: and Christianity does not seem to be there. A cry to all the churches rises up from the heart of modern man: "Come to us where we are. Help us to make the passage into the coming technocratic age without falling into the despair and brutality of a new paganism. Teach us sincere respect and affection for our fellow men. If the charity of the Good Samaritan burns in your hearts, show that you share our desires and aspirations. In our struggle to build the city of man, we need the support which your faith and hope alone can give. If you remain comfortably in your churches and cloisters, we are much afraid that God will become a stranger to modern life. Christianity, secluded in a world of its own, will turn into a mere relic to be cherished by a few pious souls."[6]

The future begins with today's children. We must search for ways to transcend the divisions of the present moment. There must be a serious converging of those parents, theologians, educators, pastors, and good men and women everywhere to invest in the future of our holy doubters, our praying atheists. We cannot provide them with a totally supportive environment but we can be there with many of them to affirm their quest, their humanity and their image of God.

Grace

Up to this point most of my words and your reactions have focused on what *we* can do to bring about the spiritual formation of the children of our age. In these last few sentences we must recognize that something completely independent of our efforts is also involved here. In fact the major force at work in the process is beyond our ability to manipulate, control or influence. It would be appropriate to label it "grace," that is, God's self-communication to us and to our moment in history, by which we are able to realize and fulfill our Christianity and our humanity.

The very fact of our existence means that God's presence and support are available to us. As it was put in Vatican II's *Lumen Gentium:*

> The Spirit dwells in the Church and in the hearts of the faithful as in a temple (n. 4).

When we are working together God is always with us.

When working with children we often see little miracles. We usually act as if we or the child made these miracles happen. We undertake the responsibility for making sure that they happen again. This is a heavy burden. We forget about grace.

We can avoid defining this much fought-over term "grace." It is sufficient for our purposes to say that there is some kind of love affair between God and the child which has operative and cooperative aspects. Bernard Lonergan in describing the process of conversion says:

> For Christians it is God's love flooding our hearts through the Holy Spirit given to us. It is the gift of grace, and since the days of Augustine, a distinction has been drawn between operative and cooperative grace. Operative grace is the replacement of the heart of stone by a heart of flesh, a replacement beyond the horizon of the heart of stone. Cooperative grace is the heart of flesh becoming effective in good works through human freedom. Operative grace is religious conversion. Cooperative grace is the effectiveness of conversion, the gradual movement toward a full and complete transformation of the whole of one's living and feeling, one's thoughts, words, deeds and omissions.[7]

We can soften the theological language by considering the pagan goddesses known as "The Graces." They were so-named because they brought to mind the pleasant beauty, the "grace," of the fertile field or garden. The analogy is relevant to our spiritual concerns. When we plant a seed we take care to choose the right kind, to prepare the soil, to irrigate, to protect from frost, to weed, to fertilize. Then there is growth. But in actuality we are only cooperating with a miraculous process by which the seed turns into a plant and grows. The seed contains within it all of the history of its species and the potential for the future of its kind. In a fantastic way totally out of our control the seed relates to the soil, the air and its own mysterious interior environment. We can kill it or help it but in no way can we bear the full responsibility for the process.

When it comes to the spiritual formation of our children we often forget that we did not create the seed nor the process. Probably we have less power over the spiritual growth of our children than we have with a plant in our garden.

Spiritual reality is not to be found in these printed pages. If the hand that closes this book will also find the warm little hand of one of God's children, then some of what has been written here will come alive.

When you and a child walk together, God walks with you.

APPENDICES

Some After Words

The two appendices relate but are not integral to the major points in this book. Appendix B, *Beyond Faith Development: Some Reflections on Religious Education,* is from the right hand. It is an attempt to put this book into context for a professional religious educator. Appendix A, on *Haiku Writing: From Caterpillars to Butterflies,* is quite a left-handed exercise, and shares my tool of last resort. All who are concerned with the spiritual formation of themselves or others usually reserve an apparatus for those frequent "when all fails" situations. Haiku has been mine, personally, and when working with others, for the past twenty years.

Appendix A
Haiku Writing:
From Caterpillars to Butterflies

Greek philosophers talk about people being caught in the tension between an eternal background and a temporal foreground. There is in each of us the gross groveler, preoccupied with petty details. But we also contain a divine spark which calls us to lofty heights. Some Zen Buddhists refer to this situation as "little mind" and "big mind." "Big" is not used because we have great intellectual thoughts but because we are invited to participate in experience which is bigger than our own preoccupations. To use the language of some Christian mystics: Sometimes we are able to use God's eyes to look at things.

Finding the Divine within the ordinary is to attempt to see life as a sacrament, and this is an especially strong contemporary tendency.

We are all required to be caterpillars during much of our daily lives. This is equally true in the lives of our children. But there are also opportunities to be butterflies. Picking up the habit of looking for these opportunities when young will refresh us through the years that come. I have encouraged both adults and children to play with haiku as a stepping-stone to spiritual growth. Children need very little introduction, usually just a few words and some encouragement. We should not be too concerned about the technical rules of the game. What is written here is primarily for the use of adults as well as an incentive to interpret this process for the children with whom they have contact.

I
BEGINNING TO WRITE HAIKU

Over the past four hundred years haiku writing has become a recognized form of poetry in Japan. For some people haiku is an end in itself. For others it is part of a spiritual discipline or a means to heighten awareness of nature. Others write haiku because it is simply waiting there to be written. The best way to understand haiku is to write some haiku, which, like all poetry, is not a product but simply the recording of a process.

In Japan there are many rules and conventions for haiku. There are a number of schools, each with its own particular approach. It is important to bind yourself by some rules. Your creative effort is like a seed. It must bloom where it is planted. If it keeps changing its environment it will not develop properly.

For those who look to haiku as a tool for slowing down and becoming more in tune with life, I suggest they start with only three rules:

(1) Write a poem with seventeen syllables and divided into three lines. The first line has five syllables, the second has seven, the third has five.
(2) Let the poem reflect the season of the year.
(3) Don't be clever!

1. Seventeen Syllables—Three Lines

When Japanese is translated into English, it is sometimes put into four lines rather than three. It has been suggested that this would be a better arrangement for writing haiku in English. Also, haiku is an outgrowth of the Japanese language, which has no article and practically no pronouns. There is no punctuation in Japanese haiku. Punctuation is, to some extent, replaced by words called *kireji*. These differences have led some to suggest that haiku is not an appropriate form of English writing. Despite all this, the writing of haiku in English has proved a rich experience for many people.

The person who introduced me to haiku used a name which was translated "Seventeen Stepping-Stones." Arrange these stones in three lines (five syllables, seven syllables, five syllables) and you may walk into many an interesting river.

You should let each line express separate parts of your haiku. Do not express two thoughts which meet in the middle of the second line.

2. Reflect the Season

Haiku is a form of listening. Therefore, it is not a mental construction as much as it is an attempt to overcome our separateness from our natural surroundings. There is always a temptation to indulge our self-centeredness and write about the world's relationship to us. Nothing can stop you if you prefer to look at your individual problems or achievements, but if you are attempting to overcome your separateness you will find it helpful to always have the poem indicate the season of the year. Sometimes this is done by simply naming the season or month:

Through the long summer
the tall brown meadow grass will
bow and bow and bow.

At other times the season is just present in the nature of the poem.

All the rules are simply to help us slow down and listen. We should not try to create a "great poem." The Shakers have a saying:

Open the windows
And the doors and receive
Whomsoever is sent.

Do not try to compose haiku—just open the windows and doors and look at whatever comes. The world is your classroom; sit and wait for your teacher. In the seventeenth century, Matsuo Basho gave some strong advice to haiku writers:

Go to the pine if you want to learn about the pine, or to the bamboo if you want to learn about the bamboo. And in doing so, you must leave your subjective preoccupation with yourself. Otherwise you impose yourself on the object and do not learn. Your poetry issues of its own accord when you and the object have become one—when you have plunged deep enough into the object to see something like a hidden glimmering there. However well phrased your poetry may be, if your feeling is not natural—if the object and yourself are separate—then your poetry is not true poetry but merely your subjective counterfeit.[1]

3. Don't Be Clever

The third rule follows on Basho's advice. Be yourself; avoid the temptation to impress yourself or anyone else. In this way there is no such thing as a good or bad haiku. The only question is whether or not it is honest. Poetry is simply being yourself.

There is another seventeen-syllable form of poetry called *senryu*. It was designed to let people show how clever they are at commenting upon the human condition. But this is not haiku as I am thinking of it.

In order to encourage authenticity, haiku masters suggested a number of guidelines. Some of them were:

a. Use everyday language.
b. Look for haiku in small ordinary experiences.
c. Try to discover the unity of all around you and within you.
d. Say things in a simple way and develop one thought at a time.
e. Be natural. Do not write for an audience.

Also remember, if you are tenaciously holding onto an idea and trying to squeeze it into seventeen syllables, there is probably too much of you in the poem. It may be hard to accept until you have written haiku for a while, but honest poems just seem to flow naturally like water between rocks. If you are trying too hard, you are not listening.

Collecting Your Haiku

It is a good idea to get a little book in which to keep your haiku. A small artist's sketchbook is an inexpensive and durable notebook. Most of my haiku occurs when I am sitting out in the fields or during a stroll in the woods. I try to remember to have some paper with me. At the end of the day I take my scraps of paper and enter the haiku in my book. Sometimes I go for months between haiku, yet there is still a stream. Most people record the date after the poem; some put the time of day.

It is important to keep all your haiku, even the "bad" ones. For haiku is a way of exploring your inner world and you do not always hear what you are saying for a few days, weeks, or even years.

We can usually find different levels of meaning in a haiku poem. People sometimes assume that a haiku master chooses a piece of nature in order to make a profound philosophical point. This is putting things backward. There are no profound parts of life; there are only little moments. But if you focus on something little it becomes large. Also, where you are psychologically and spiritually will determine what you can see or hear. If we are truly honest in expressing our relationship to the natural world, there may be double or quadruple levels of meaning, simply because we are touching the life process. Life is like an onion; there are many layers. When you peel back one layer, another becomes apparent. You should not try to write with secondary meaning or any meaning at all; that is only cleverness and can poison your well.

There is much to be learned from your haiku. The lessons are not always apparent. One day before I followed the monastic life I was wrestling with some major decisions about which crossroad to take in my life. The matter had been turned over often in my head and discussed with family and close friends. I was not ready to face that I simply had to make a decision. I attempted to lose myself in the preparations for a weekend gathering of professional colleagues. Here we were to get a sharp focus on the problems of the world and look at all kinds of organizational and personal concerns. Just before I left home I was sitting by the fireplace and a cricket walked out on the hearth. I watched him for a few moments. Then I drove a couple of hours to a country lodge. Shortly after I arrived all the participants gathered together. It was evening. The light was dim. The mood was rather solemn. In the quiet before we began, a cricket walked out into the middle of the floor. I wrote:

Here deep in the woods
I am found by the cricket
who lives in my house.

The haiku and the image of the cricket stayed within my head during the meeting. Some time later, I really heard what I had written. It was no different here than at home. I knew what the issues were. The decision had to be made.

Sometimes I think it is presumptuous to talk about "writing" haiku. Often I feel more like a clumsy medium at a séance. If I can detach sufficiently from my self-centeredness, I can be an instrument for some nourishing poems.

Writing with Other People

A haiku is a very individual thing, but there are many advantages to writing and sharing these poems with others. It helps people to experience each other in different dimensions. Children especially take to group sessions.

Whenever haiku is shared verbally it should be repeated. It is hard to hear on the first reading. It is better to write it on the blackboard if one is available. Also, there should be a minute or two of quiet in between each haiku that is shared.

There is a special attitude in writing haiku with other people. Apparently, haiku masters would frequently meet with students and others to write together. They would compose little books of poems.

Sometimes when writing with other people I find a great increase in my own awareness of life around me. Frequently the sessions begin with a brief sharing of memories of little things we have seen during the day. Then we each write a poem or two and share these. As I hear someone else's haiku it awakens a feeling inside of me and I jump into similar pools, but with my own peculiar splash.

I know no better way to turn a yearly leaf than to spend an afternoon writing and sharing. It is a good way to spend a part of the last day of the year or a birthday. Long after the wrapping paper and gifts are gone these haiku will bring back our moments together.

Sharing haiku can also be a way of checking in with each other. Once I was part of a group which came together for a special meal each week. We each brought some food and a haiku. Before we would begin to eat we would share our haiku as a way of letting our lives touch each other.

Following the Rules

Does everyone always follow the guidelines I have set out above? No. Do I? No. But I wish I did.

The one important rule is to live a life that lets you experience something of your inner quiet every day. Then, as Basho tells us, we return "to the world of our daily experience to seek therein the truth of beauty. No matter what we may be doing at a given moment, we must not forget that it has a bearing upon our everlasting self which is poetry."

II
THE LITERATURE OF HAIKU

Before Basho

From early times there was a form of poetry called *tanka* (or *waka*). It was composed of thirty-one syllables. The poem was divided into five lines with the following syllables: 5-7-5-7-7. When more than one person contributed to the poem, such poetry was called *renga* or "linked verse." These poems were chains; each link was to be poetically related to the preceding verse. There could be as many as a hundred links. At the imperial court there was the practice of giving the 5-7-5 part (*hokku* or "starting verse") and then having a competition to see who could supply the best remaining two lines (7-7). This was sometimes called "verse capping." It is still the custom for haiku writers to link verses, i.e., for several poets to supply alternate poems when they are writing together.

In the thirteenth century poets began to simply write a poem of 5-7-5 syllables. This was the beginning of *haiku.* The first haiku were called "sporting verse" or *"haikkai renga."* These early poems were often crude and shallow. Others were genuinely humorous. The poets were attempting to outdo each other's cleverness. The situation gradually improved until the stage was set in the seventeenth century for the entrance of Basho and the great masters who followed him. Now a spiritual significance was being sensed in the "one breath poems" focusing on a single moment in life.

Four Haiku Masters

What follows are a few poems and comments on four poets: Basho, Buson, Issa, and Shiki. The poems are not really translations but quasi-literal renderings which let the reader get a brief whiff of the poet's genius.

To give you some idea of what you are missing, let me take this old Shaker hymn:

'Tis the gift to be simple.
'Tis the gift to be free.
'Tis the gift to come down where we ought to be.
And when we find ourselves in the place just right
'Twill be in the valley of love and delight!

Applying the same criteria (or lack of them!) used in the haiku that follows, the Shaker hymn would be rendered something like this:

Being simple is a gift
And so is being free
It is also a gift to ground oneself in an appropriate place
Which, when it is discovered,
Will be found to be a delightful spot between the hills.

No attempt has been made to render these poems into seventeen English syllables, though, of course, in Japanese they are seventeen syllables.

MATSUO BASHO
(1644–1694)

Basho is the most famous name in haiku. He began writing poetry when he was nine years old. When he was twenty-two he commenced his instruction in the spiritual discipline of Buddhism at the monastery of Koyasan. At thirty-five he wrote a new sytle of his own making.

For Basho all art started in the simple cradle of nature.

> The beginning of Culture:
> in the center of the country
> a rice-planting-song.

There was a unity in what he saw and wrote. The most famous haiku ever written came spontaneously from Basho's lips. He was sitting quietly in his garden when he heard a splash. To him, it was all one thing, a "frog-jump-in-water-sound."

> "Old pond" equals—
> a frog-jump-in-
> water-sound.

This great poet took literally to the spiritual path. Much of his life was spent in simple walking journeys. Some of these were of great distance. He began the first of these trips when he was forty. Traveling was often difficult and precarious. Yet these journeys were necessary to Basho in his attempt to detach from self-centeredness and to merge with the totality of life. No matter how high he traveled he was searching for a simple life.

> On the mountain path,
> what is this special thing?
> A simple violet.

His quiet travels were part of the spiritual discipline which helped Basho be there at those quick moments when life unfurls.

> On the mountain road
> first the scent of plums, then suddenly—
> the sunrise!

Basho's roads were both an outer and inner experience. They are roads we all vaguely recognize.

This road:
with no one walking on it,
autumn nightfall.

Here we find that special loneliness which the Japanese term *sabi* combined with a poverty of expression and symbol (*wabi*) that, rather than taking a panoramic view, goes deep into life. It is this sharp focusing on the simple which seems to produce the unique spiritual restfulness.

Basho died on a trip, among his friends and disciples. This was his final poem.

Taken ill on a journey
but still my dreams roam
over the dried up fields.

TANIGUCHI BUSON
(1715–1783)

Buson followed close behind Basho in time and talent. He was also a famous painter. Unlike Basho, Buson had a secular outlook. Neither does he closely identify himself with the human condition as did Issa. He weaves his words into poems with excellent craftsmanship. Buson rarely exhibited the personal intensity of Basho or Issa. He stepped back a bit and became a brilliant observer.

Morning haze—
like a painting of a dream,
people pass by.

He felt that working too hard at things got in the way of poetry and living. Most of his fellow poets approached spring blossoms as a challenge to their talents, but not Buson.

I come to the blossoms
and go to sleep under the tree—
free time!

Yet, sometimes the whole world is contained in the sharp eye of this painter-poet.

The spring rains fall
and on the roof being soaked
is a cloth hand-ball!

YATARO KOBAYASHI
ISSA
(1763–1826)

I would have liked to have taken long and frequent walks with this poet. He found God everywhere.

Here at my old house
I see the face of God
in the face of the snail.

Above all, Issa was a man, a very human man. He knew sorrow all his life. Nothing ever seemed to go right for him. When Issa was two, his mother died. Five years later his father remarried. Then began a forty-year struggle with his stepmother. His memories of childhood were unpleasant ones. Issa was worked hard and beaten often. All his life he identified with the weak and helpless, be they children, flies, or sparrows.

Come, you can
play with me!—
orphaned sparrow.

When he was thirteen he went to Edo (Tokyo). While there he began to study haiku. In his late twenties he decided to commit himself to religion and to poetry. It was then that he chose the name "Issa" which means a "cup of tea." He saw himself as simple and ordinary, like a cup of tea. Like the tea he felt his work would vanish in a moment.

Distant mountains
reflect in the jeweled eyes
of the dragonfly!

Issa was a priest of the Jodo Shinshu sect of Buddhism, which was much less austere than Zen. It emulated Buddha Amida who refused to enter Nirvana until his merit was so great that those who would call upon his name would also be able to enter "The Pure Land" (Jodo).

For ten years Issa traveled on long journeys. Like Basho he traveled to overcome his attachment to self and worldly things.

> A sudden shower, equals
> being naked
> on a naked horse.

When Issa was fifty (1813) an understanding was finally reached with his stepmother. Happy, but in ill health, he returned to his village and the old farmhouse where he had been born. He married a village girl named Kiku. She was twenty-seven. They wanted children very badly. Kiku bore several children, all of whom died young. There was great sorrow here. One little daughter, Sato, brought Issa a special joy. She died of smallpox before she was two. Issa wrote that Sato closed her eyes as the morning glory closed its blossoms. He loved children and renewed himself by smiling at them.

> Melting snow
> makes the village brim-full:
> of children!

Of all the animals and insects with whom Issa identified, toads and frogs seemed to be the closest to his heart.

> He who appears now
> is Lord Toad
> of this thicket!

Whatever its failing, it is *his* thicket! This old toad can give all of us courage.

Throughout his troubled life Issa was looking for beauty. Even his young wife was to die, leaving him once more alone. Often he had to detach from tribulations that would have drowned weaker men.

Loveliness is
looking through a tear in a shoji screen
and seeing the milky way.

Shortly before his death his house burned down. He spent his last days in a storage shed without windows and with holes in the roof. He could see the mid-winter sky which symbolized his lifelong search for "The Pure-Land." His final poem was found under his pillow after his death.

Again, I give thanks—
The snow on the bed quilt,
it also comes from God.

MASAOKA SHIKI
(1867–1902)

Life and haiku became rather artificial in nineteenth century Japan. It was hard for a brilliant and restless young man like Shiki to find anything in which to believe. Everything rang false. In his poems we feel the deep awareness of a poet preoccupied with hypocrisy.

Shiki was something of an iconoclast. When still a young poet he attacked the cult of Basho. He demanded a hard rationalism. Yet, it was not a comfort to him.

In the autumn wind
I find no gods
and no Buddhas.

Shiki gave voice to the beginning of whatever age we are in now. It is neither old nor new, real nor unreal. Many paths present themselves. Decisions are not easy.

In the moonlight
the wild geese fly low
over the railroad tracks.

Not all that is new lives, and not all that is old is dead.

In a forgotten pot
a flower blooms—
spring day!

Shiki was a sharp critic of those who attempted to reduce haiku and life to rules and prizes. His main advice was to forget the rules and be natural.

The skylark school
and the frog school—
argue over singing.

Shiki died from tuberculosis at the age of thirty-five. He had great pain and spent much of his last years in bed. Life had a bitter-sweet quality to this poet who stands between us and the earlier haiku masters.

People go home
after the fireworks.
How dark it is!

The light in the next room
also goes out:
the night is cold!!

III
TEACHING HAIKU TO CHILDREN

As was stated at the beginning, children require very little introduction. The best way to begin is to simply read some haiku, talk about it and encourage the youngsters to share the feelings and imagery they experience as they hear the poem. Next, go outside with them; walk, observe the woods or the garden. Then ask them to write. They should be introduced to the 5-7-5 pattern, but it should not be overemphasized.

One of the most precious gifts I ever received came many years ago from my young adopted daughter. She had been born in the Orient in a war-torn land. Although she was by now thoroughly Americanized, she still maintained a quiet inner space, which I believe reflected in what she wrote this particular afternoon. She had joined some adult friends writing haiku on my birthday. After giving it a try she shyly handed me her poem as one would hand someone a flower. It reflected much about herself and about me, but I think it also said something about the world from which she came:

One little blossom
On a plum tree in winter
Alone, cold and wet.

IV
LITURGICAL HAIKU

Often in the busyness associated with festivals people can lose the meaning through their hectic pace. An interesting project for an individual, group, or family is to select a few moments at important times in their year to write haiku. It has the tendency of quieting us down, making us become more aware, letting God grab us. There is an additional advantage of telling us something about our spiritual experience, which we are often unable to see for some time.

Advent
Steaming hot tea mug
on a frosty window sill,
a now-memory.

The tall Christmas tree
stands quietly observing
the busy people.

Christmas
The bright Christmas star
reflects in the soft brown eyes
of the silent boy.

Lent
The lonely bird calls
into the unknown silence
searching for a mate.

The dirty gardener
is showered with plum petals
while he meditates.

Palm Sunday
On waking I hear
a crow calling as she flies—
Holy Week begins.

Easter
A new spring flower
quietly blooms in the ruins
of the burned cabin.

Pentecost
Silently it comes
in the early light of dawn
the first squash blossom!

V

BOOKS ON HAIKU

There are a growing number of haiku books in English. I would especially recommend the following:

Harold G. Henderson, *An Introduction to Haiku* (Garden City, New York: Doubleday Anchor Books, 1958).
This is a good anthology from before Basho to Shiki. The author's translations are fine renderings of the spirit of the poem as well as the literal meaning. Each poet is introduced with a good review of his life and poetry.

Matsuo Basho, *The Narrow Road to the Deep North and Other Travel Sketches,* translated and with an introduction by Nobuyuki Yuasa (Baltimore: Penguin Books, 1966).

This is the story of five of Basho's journeys written in the *haibon* style, i.e., a mixture of haiku and prose. "The Narrow Road to the Deep North" is the final selection and is illustrated with small paintings by Buson.

Issa, *The Year of My Life,* translated and with an introduction by
> Nobuyuki Yuasa (Berkeley: University of California Press,
> 1960 and 1972).

Issa collected many poems and prose comments into twenty-one chapters which span an imaginary year of his life.

Cliff Edwards, *Everything Under Heaven: The Life and Words*
> *of a Nature Mystic, Issa of Japan* (Richmond: Virginia Com-
> monwealth University, 1980). Also two private editions,
> *Haiku Talk* and *Torn Banana Leaves* (New York: Kyoto East
> Haiku Society).

Cliff Edwards presents a well-grounded and personal Christian reaction to the spirituality of haiku which makes his work especially valuable to me. His book on Issa is outstanding. In *Haiku Talk* he collaborates with Mariyana Shizuko, a Japanese journalist and artist. *Torn Banana Leaves* is a fascinating "haiku journal" of his father, a self-taught radio technician, who after his wife's death went to the Canary Islands and took up haiku. Edwards also uses the haiku of grade school students in his publication.

VI
HAIKU AND SPIRITUAL GROWTH

The use of haiku has only an indirect relation to any single topic in this book. However, it can be valuable to the overall process of spiritual growth in at least two ways.

First, it is a good place to go when we get lost on the journey. Meister Eckhart tells those who have lost God to go back to where they last saw him—in other words, to stop frantically trying one thing after another. Like a lost child in the woods, it is better to stand still and be found. Haiku helps us do that.

With specific reference to the spiritual growth of children, haiku is also a good bridge between everyday life and the development of spiritual awareness.

I have never known haiku writing to harm anyone. For these times when there is no specialized medication we can think of, it is an old-fashioned broad spectrum remedy which can be applied to a variety of spiritual ills. It is also pleasurable even when there is no excuse to do it at all.

Appendix B
Beyond Faith Development:
Some Reflections
on Religious Education

Not all of us who are Christian educators are professional religious educators. However, I have some observations which may resonate with the experience of those in religious education.

First of all, I have been surprised at the extremely broad spectrum of religious educators. There are graduates from academic theology programs on one end, and well-meaning high school sophomores on the other. Additionally, there are those sensitive to contemporary theological works in the same area with those who paraphrase the Baltimore Catechism. A major issue has been succinctly put by a local religious education coordinator who said, "It all boils down to whether or not a person believes there should be any change from the way we used to teach in the 1950's."

A second general observation is that, despite a growing consensus on the limitations of the classroom model, alternatives are slow in developing. A partial evolution is taking place in youth and young adult ministeries, where the discussion group model is normal. Among the pre-adolescents no one is satisfied with the classroom approach, and yet by default it continues to be used. In my opinion this is associated to some extent with a general discouragement about religious education among younger children. I suspect that many would agree with the blunt pastor of a large parish in a northwest city who said recently:

> We tried religious education for public school children for about three years until 1978. It did not work. The parents just didn't seem to care. At first, we would get about a dozen children. Then after a few weeks they would just quit coming and there would be a teacher with no one to teach. The parents did not even come to Mass. So I guess expecting them to send their children to religious education was a bit much.

I have listened to teachers in a parochial school system express views not far removed from the pastor's point.

Third, catechists have in general a wonderful *esprit de corps.* The present religious education system would have to be judged successful if on no other grounds than what it has done for the life and faith of the catechists. Coming from this excellent and giving spirit have been many advantages, not the least of which is a change in the entire concept of Christian ministry.

The teachers seem to be cooperative about approaches to take; in fact they are anxious to have a clear directive. However, those assigned to working with pre-adolescent children often express some difficulty. If the theoretical models of religious education in their area emphasize such ordinary aspects as theology, scriptural studies, sacramental preparation, moral education and conscience development, there is frequent concern about how to apply these points to younger children. Furthermore, when people such as myself suggest that the central focus in the pre-adolescent period ought to be spiritual growth, the religious educator can be somewhat overwhelmed. They are already asked to do a wide variety of tasks. At the present time the parish director of religious education is expected to give a sort of catechetical direction to the entire parish community. The thought of being assigned in addition as spiritual director of ten to a thousand children is just too much to expect.

A final observation concerns students and parents. The pre-adolescent religious instruction in Confraternity of Christian Doctrine (CCD) classes and to a lesser extent in full-time school settings is not satisfying to anyone. Largely this is a subjective deduction. However, the current sociological studies of "drop-outs" support this observation to some extent. Among older dropouts (presumably not those expressing the normal doubt aspects of the faith pilgrimage) the Hoge study shows that "ninety-eight percent of the older dropouts had received religious training as children; fifty-nine percent had attended Catholic schools."[1] There also seems to be a growing number of parents, not a few on the fringe of the Church, searching for alternatives for the traditional Christian education models.

I suggest that one of the factors contributing to this frustrating situation with the education of young children has been a disabling dialectic. First we had the catechism (or "Bible study" among Protestants) approach. The antithesis to this was presented by the faith development school, which was often presented to the grass-roots catechists as an endless list of things not to do.

The thesis of this book is that (1) pre-adolescent education is essential to later development, (2) it should primarily be "spiritual" and not "religious" (see Chapters 2 and 3 for distinctions), (3) parents or parent substitutes are the most effective catechists, (4) the role of the religious education coordinator should be to provide support and training to parents and others attempting to be guides to their children, and (5) this function should be a high priority for a religious educator, even when the number of parents undertaking this responsibility represents only a small percentage of the total parish population.

Against this background I would like to raise some fundamental questions about faith development as it has been applied at the local level.

Ronald Goldman asked, "Must we give up religious education before the age of twelve, or is there a positive alternative we can offer?" If there is a clear answer to this question it certainly has not been adequately communicated from within the faith development school.

Faith Development:
A Progressive Education Trap for Religious Educators?
In a legitimate attempt to make religious education more relevant, and cognizant that children were "turning off" in

droves, we insisted that catechists not view children as "little adults." The result has been the establishment of some fairly rigid concepts which are interpreted in a needlessly restrictive way in many cases. We like to begin with Piaget, who, in describing the cognitive ability of children, said that there is a pre-operational stage (2–7 years) which he termed "intuitive." This is followed by a concrete operational stage (7–11 years), meaning that a child is cognitively able to comprehend very specific situations. Finally (after 12), there is an operational stage in which children can understand concepts. As brilliant and revolutionary as Piaget's concepts were at the time, he was talking (1) of a different age and culture, and (2) of an intellectual framework.

Ronald Goldman used Piaget's concepts out of a concern for what he thought was an inappropriate cognitive program being developed in England. He developed his own sense of the pre-religious stage (ages 5–7), the sub-religious stage (ages 7–9), and the personal religious stage (ages 9–12), and the religious (13 and up). Goldman was specifically attacking the practice of teaching scriptural passages. He was pointing to a gap in comprehension between the teacher and the child. If we insist on cognitive theological concepts being shoved at children, then the only way these concepts can be accepted by the child is in the general realm of the fairy tale. These will become easily rejected when a person reaches adulthood. Goldman advocates instead "life themes" and suggests that Jesus himself did the same. I support Goldman's reaction against Christian education being approached in an entirely intellectual fashion at an early age.

In this country came the strong influence of Lawrence Kohlberg, as interpreted by James Fowler. Kohlberg uses Piaget's concepts in the specific area of moral development. This has resulted in a problem in education in general which has recently been under attack from psychologists outside the developmental ranks. The following analysis by Bob Samples is a case in point:

> In no way are these words intended to denigrate the intuitive or the rational genius of Piaget, but rather to criticize the vivid use to which a rationally dominant culture puts such work. Some psychologists, such as Lawrence Kohlberg

at Harvard, say Piaget's constructs are so viable that they relate to moral growth. Kohlberg's work is little more than a shift in content that confirms Piaget's hierarchical stages. Kohlberg substitutes abstract moral questions for the abstract logical questions that characterize Piaget's tasks. His stages of moral growth include six stages paralleling Piaget's four. His conclusions are painfully predictable. Children who are adept at abstract manipulation of linear physical concepts are also adept at the abstract manipulation of linear moral concepts. Kohlberg, it appears, further fails to recognize that the bias toward moral linearity is as culturally affected as is the bias toward physical linearity. Logic is its own reward; it creates internal consistency regardless of content.

The pity of this is that Kohlberg maintains that humans cannot be morally operative unless they are at the formal operations stage of Piaget. Culturally this would probably exclude all Hopi, Zuni, Swahili, Maori and Eskimos. The basis for this exclusion would be technical rather than theoretical. Each of these cultures has no formal abstract symbolic language. Thus their cultures do not create a mechanism for them to practice abstract reasoning and therefore score well on the tests of Kohlberg or Piaget.

Theoretically neither Piaget nor Kohlberg could allow this condition to be considered moral—theorists must somehow be accountable to those excluded by their theories as well as those included.

The metaphoric mind includes rationality, linearity, and logic—for it created them. But like some children, the rational mind often seems embarrassed by the presence of its parents.[2]

The recent interest in neo-Freudian concepts such as those of Erik Erikson is probably an improvement (see Chapter 4). The approach is certainly less cognitive, and more inclusive of such areas as trust, intimacy, community, friendship, wisdom, etc. All of these attitudes have their place. But they too can be misapplied. The frequency with which terms are bantered around leads one to worry that there is a desire on the part of some for oversimplification in the guise of establishing "practical guidelines" for armies of catechists who need to have some kind of objective framework. The process of education is basically a subjective process. It has to do with some kind of spark passing in a generally undefinable fashion between a teacher and a student. And this is true whether that teacher be a parent, religious educator, pastor, or another child. The failure to recognize this dynamic raises the danger in the spiritual realm of creating the horrors of the general field of education where we are continually bombarded with non-communication in the form of pseudo-scientific jargon. As more than one critic of modern education has suggested, putting a name on a problem is not solving the problem.[3]

When psychological concepts are applied to religious education, they are, in most cases, gross oversimplifications of theories which were never meant to be universally applied. We can appreciate our common tendency to want to work with certainty. But we should also realize that true educational opportunities come when we step out of our little guidelines in order to reach toward that dynamic and grace-filled moment in which a child opens to life.

No developmental theory should ever be applied unreservedly to a specific individual. The theories are based upon large segments and they do not tell you when a particular human being is going to change, or in precisely what direction. The exact same stages of development in one person are seldom, if ever, followed in another.

There has been an unfortunate tendency to label. In a review of the criticism of the Kohlberg/Fowler approach, theologian Richard McBrien cites the over-emphasis on rationality, on justice alone (not being concerned sufficiently with other aspects of the human quest, such as intimacy, community, friendship), and a one-sided concept of faith as a fundamental attitude (in contrast to content). McBrien then goes on to say that there is an objection in addition to

    ... the tendency of this approach's adherents to "typecast" their fellow Christians as if these stages were evaluative rather than descriptive and particular rather than general.[4]

There is another danger we should learn from past mistakes. We sometimes look at children in a way similar to how early anthropologists looked at "lower levels" of civilization found in different parts of the world. We start with a concept that where we are is the highest stage. Then we look at all other experience in terms of how long it will take others to reach our position. We now know that when this attitude was applied among the missionaries in Africa, enormous sections of valuable spirituality were wiped away because they did not fit into the developmental framework. And only now, after many painful years, are these indigenous concepts being rewoven into the fabric of the African Christian's life.

In a similar way, we can look upon young children as undeveloped phenomena which will hopefully evolve into our image. For example, in a recent abbreviated explanation of developmental theories, we are told that trust *only* develops at the infantile stage, self-mastery *only* between the ages of 2 and 3, and a controlled creativity *only* between 4 and 6. The child "actively engages in the task of modern society" *only* between the ages of 7 and 10, integrates his personal experience with "our future task within Christianity" *only* at ages 11–18, begins to make responsible commitments to others *only* between ages 19–25, develops a concern for the future of Christianity *only* after the age of 25, and *only* "culminates in the later stages of life by focusing on the ultimate meaning in the midst of the limiting boundaries of our life-cycle." This attitude comes from the perspective of someone standing at the end of the scale looking back on everything and everyone in terms of how long it would take them to catch up. Such a statement would not have been written by anyone in his or her twenties.

There is certainly a positive side to faith development, in its concern that we not attempt to cram cognitive concepts into a child's head. But the negative side, as often applied, is a pseudo-scientific judgment which fails to take into account individual differences in the dynamic of growth. This is especially evident when theorists totally fail to take into account that there is anything other than the cognitive in Christian education, leading to statements such as the following (from a manual for catechists):

> It is better to leave the child alone for his first couple years. He has enough to do to get his sensory-motor apparatus in control and functioning. He's trying to find out what is him and what isn't him, whether the blanket is part of his hand or part of the bed.

I find this suggestion chilling. This frigid jargon seems to deny the sacramental basis of Christian life. At that remarkable time of life when a child has not yet followed our adult example to crawl inside of our separate identities and to hug our body shells around us in splendid loneliness, there is an opportunity for contact with God which is indeed unique, and probably never again duplicated.

To lead a child to find the divine in the ordinary moments of life should be something that is second nature to us. We are greatly impressed by what happens in the spiritual training of young children in primitive societies or in Buddhistic cultures where all of the little adventures of early childhood are seen as having spiritual dimensions. We, on the other hand, suggest to our teachers that we simply, "leave the child alone for his first couple years."

Unfortunately, this type of situation is not new. We have experienced it in the fiasco of progressive education, begun by well-meaning reformers like John Dewey, who was, according to education critic George Leonard, "seduced" by the psychology of his time. The result was a generation of teachers who waited for children to exhibit manifestations of readiness or interest before teaching them. This, according to Leonard, resulted in the student's capacity for learning being seriously under-rated. This state of affairs was reinforced by the developmental psychologists after Dewey. Leonard counts as worthless the studies which show what children cannot do until certain ages. "It is," he says, "as cruel to bore a child as to beat him."[5]

It is important to avoid this unnecessary repetition of history in Christian education.

Beyond Faith Development

Quite a number of post-faith development methods have been put forward which would avoid the progressive education trap. The following represent five that have some especial relevance to what is discussed in this book:

1. *Community.* An emerging concept concerns the interrelation of the child to community. This is especially meaningful to the younger child. A primary voice in this country in this area is the Episcopalian John Westerhoff,[6] who calls for a community with four definite chracteristics:

A. The community has a clear identity. It is "a self-conscious, intentional community of faith."

B. A community is "small enough to have meaningful interaction," by which he specifically means that the community must be under three hundred members.

C. There must be in this community a three-generational level. He calls the older generation the generation of "memory"; the younger generation is the generation of "vision," and the parent generation is the generation of the "present."

D. The true community must have some means of uniting all of the diverse groups within the community—specifically, the gifts of apostles, prophets and teachers.

The application of these four criteria is helpful in several ways. They can be used to distinguish between truly emerging communities and simply enjoyable but shallow experiences. A weekend retreat with a groovy priest where the kids can use the opportunity to focus upon their particular interests at the moment is not community. There must be the introduction of the generation of "vision" to the generation of "memories" and of the "present." Most important, there must be a tie-in to the Gospel message. Simply making a session interesting so that youngsters will want to come back is not enough.

Most would agree that the religious education and the spiritual growth of a child will develop rather naturally in a community environment such as Westerhoff envisions. Such an ideal community, like the family itself, would have little need for concepts of faith development. They would simply proceed unconsciously in a generally constructive trial and error system.

The difficulty is that the CCD teacher or even the classroom teacher is not functioning in that kind of community. Such teachers have a limited time with the children and often lack any supportive connection outside of their classroom. But the general agreement on the lack of fruitfulness of many of our religious education approaches would certainly indicate that it might be better to focus more vigorously on developing Christian community and specifically helping the child relate to that community. A casual observation of the priorities in Christian education leads me to question whether we are taking this necessity of the development of community very seriously.

The specific program put forward in this book would certainly be greatly benefited by a renewed Christian community structure. Indeed, it presupposes some kind of Gospel community, at least in the family unit.

2. *Developmental Alternatives.* Ronald Goldman and many others in both Europe and the United States have suggested that the unproductive approaches of the past be replaced by a sense of religious education developed along the lines of "life themes." Goldman specifically suggests that in the early years the process should be to find religious significance in the normal and natural experiences of children and to couple this with rather spontaneous worship services. In the middle years the children's now greatly expanded knowledge and interest would provide far more opportunities for this kind of approach. Later, more formal worship could be introduced, but always in the language of the child. When at the door of adolescence, we could begin simple biblical reflection coupled with a continuation of the life theme process and relevant worship.[7]

The practical way in which the concepts of spiritual growth in this book relate to developmental religious education of the Goldman model would probably be in the area of "worship," which Goldman defines rather broadly.

3. *Conscience Development. The National Catechetical*

Directory (NCD) has included a theory for the process of conscience formation:

> The central factor in the formation of conscience and sound moral judgment should be Christ's role in one's life. . . . His ideals, precepts, and example are present and accessible in Scripture and the tradition of the Church. To have a truly Christian conscience, one must faithfully communicate with the Lord in every phase of one's life, above all through personal prayer and through participation in the sacramental life of the Church. All other aspects of conscience formation are based on this.[8]

This is the fruit of long experience in the field of moral education in Europe, which has learned to see development of conscience in a young person as something beyond the teaching of rules and norms.

The relationship of conscience formation as reflected in the NCD to what is presented in this book is that spirituality forms the necessary foundation for the development of conscience. According to moral theologian Bernard Häring:

> Conscience produces the vital conviction in one's inner self that the attitude assumed toward the good is bound up with one's own salvation or damnation.[9]

But this sense of salvation or damnation is not a simplistic heaven or hell concept:

> It follows that conscience must be looked upon as the spiritual instinct for self-preservation, arising from the urge of complete unity and harmony. The soul craves this inner unity within herself, which is possible only through unity with the world of the true and the good.[10]

It stands to reason, therefore, that to attempt any kind of conscience formation without a solid spiritual formation is in all respects a house built on sand.

4. *Christian Roots.* There is a bottom-up reaction to the limitations of faith development which on one end of the scale is simply refusing to recognize it and tending to return to the older ways, a kind of back-to-basics approach. This is especially seen in those parishes which largely emphasize sacramental preparations. I am thinking especially of more rural parishes in which the children are simply being given a kind of "bottom line" Christianity to prepare them for the sacramental steps associated with childhood.

There is also, however, a sort of neo-theological approach developing which attempts to keep the basic right-hand context of older catechetical models, but to proceed in a more left-handed methodology. Consequently, there is also a new approach to sacramental preparation. Some of this is an attempt to introduce a child to his or her Christian roots. This represents a slight swing away from the tendency of the past decade to emphasize always the necessity of making Christianity relevant to the contemporary concerns of young people. It recognizes that the child's needs are not simply those which are new and transitory, but that there is also a need for grafting present experience onto past heritage.

It seems that the concepts presented in this book would have a place in such an approach because spiritual formation always has been a significant part of our Christian experience.

5. *Spirituality.* Spirituality for young children is a growing concern for the post-faith development period. It is here that this book would primarily be pigeonholed, although I hope that it has been demonstrated that it bears a fundamental relationship to other alternative approaches as well.

Much of what is being suggested as spirituality for young children is really a methodological approach. In contrast, the emphasis in this book is on spiritual formation. The primary emphasis should be in the home experience with substantial support provided from the religious education professionals.

The Christian community should also provide a variety of special retreats and programs designed to put a spiritual dimension on the social rite of passage from childhood to adolescence.

Notes

Chapter 1

1. Dean R. Hoge, *Converts, Dropouts, Returnees* (New York: The Pilgrim Press, 1981), pp. 83–84.

2. For example, see John Deedy, "Leadership in the United States" (quoting Avery Dulles, S.J.) in *The Tablet,* March 6, 1982, p. 221. There is a school of progressive thought which would like to see the problem of leadership almost exclusively in terms of the prohibition against married priests or women priests. Although sympathetic to both these concerns, I believe it would be naive to expect the problem of leadership to be solved by these changes. Some of these arguments are based on a rather romantic view of family life in our age.

3. *Declaration on Christian Education* (Vatican II, *Gravissimum educationis),* October 28, 1965, note 3.

4. It is sometimes suggested that this is a conservative position. Recently I heard a theologian attack the "selfishness argument" by citing a Boston pastor who has great numbers of college students volunteer when he asks for help during a sermon. Unfortunately, college students who go to Sunday Mass are not a representative group of young people. But in any event, the issue is on a much larger scale. In fact I think that young people today may well be less selfish than their elders, but that does not diminish the general problem.

5. David Villasenor, *Tapestries in Sand* (Healdsburg: Naturegraph Company, 1966), p. 102.

6. Morton T. Kelsey, *Caring: How Can We Love One Another?* (New York: Paulist Press, 1981), p. 88.

7. See Karl Rahner, *Foundations of Christian Faith* (New York: Seabury, 1978), p. 403.

8. Karl Rahner, *Concern for the Church* (New York: Crossroad Press, 1982.

9. John Paul II, encyclical letter *Redemptor hominis,* March 4, 1979, n. 1.

Chapter 2

1. Karl Rahner, *Foundations of Christian Faith* (New York: Seabury Press, 1978), pp. 6 and 16.

2. Bernard Lonergan, *Method in Theology* (New York: The Seabury Press, 1972), p. 115.

3. John Macquarrie, *Principles of Christian Theology,* 2nd ed. (New York: Charles Scribner's Sons, 1977), p. 1.

4. Unfortunately, the use of the term "existential" requires some defense in the Church today. Among some theologians left of center on the issue of social doctrine, "existentialist" is almost equivalent to "reactionary." The label connotes a disengaged privatism (and often quietism) at odds with the emerging consciousness of Christian responsibility to contribute to the health of the modern world—to indeed help to bring about the kingdom. This bizarre situation arose from the appropriation of the term "existential theology" by the school of the great German theologian and New Testament scholar, Rudolf Bultmann. Bultmann, relying on Heidegger, reacted against both an "other-worldly" fundamentalism and a liberal Christianity which merely used religion as an instrument for a changing agenda of social issues. The kingdom of God was largely God's affair and became real in the present: "God becomes real in my personal experience only by his word spoken here and now" (*Jesus Christ and Mythology,* London: SCM Press, 1958, p. 79). Although to be appreciated for many things, including its great contributions to Christian understanding of individual human existence, the Bultmann school evolved into a non-political approach. This politically conservative identification was increased through the aloofness of Gabriel Marcel and other Catholic philosophers who argued over abstract absolute values in a post-war Europe in need of provisional relief from misery.

The irony of the situation is that in the broader world view religious existentialists are quite insignificant. In the 1950's the secular existential writers often placed themselves between Christianity (extreme right) and collectivism (extreme left). A sensitivity toward the necessity of combining both the common good and the fulfillment of the individual characterized the existential attitude and is a remarkable parallel to the concerns of progressive theological and Church leaders in the 1980's.

Another uncomfortable parallel is found in the wars in the field of psychology during the 1960's. Here, the behaviorists, emphasizing environment, often reacted rigidly to humanistic psychologists exploring more wholistic approaches. Rollo May once characterized the behaviorists as "the hard hats of psychology" (certainly a rightist image), and on the progressive left of the spectrum was what was sometimes labeled "existential psychology."

In some areas of the country a fake dichotomy was carried into religious circles in ludicrous diatribes. For example, accusations were made by some theoretical "activists" that participants in encounter groups were turning their backs on world problems.

Despite all this academic confusion, the existential attitude has evolved into a significant part of many Christians' thinking, and, more important, their action. What is meant here by an existential response is simply that our hopes are based upon an understanding of existence which arises from our individual experience of human existence. It is certainly personal in the need for authenticity and the requirements for individual decision and choices in life. However, it does not require a non-political stance. In fact in Albert Camus we find a more universal appeal for revolution against oppression than among our current left-wing theologians. In *The Rebel* (*L'homme revolte,* 1951) Camus summarizes the love beneath the existential concern for justice by bringing to mind the cry of Karamazov: "If all are not saved, what good is the salvation of only one?"

A further confusion in English comes from translations of the work of another student of Heidegger, Karl Rahner, which follows the distinction in the German language between "existential," which is basic to our nature without any exercise of freedom, and "existentiell," which refers to an aspect of life which has been subjectively appropriated. The term used here, "an existential response to faith," unfortunately has aspects of both. It certainly takes place on an ontologically basic level, but is probably closer in meaning to "existentiell".

5. Bernard Lonergan, *op. cit.,* p. 117.

6. Or "kerygma."

7. Or "soteriology."

8. Or "mediation." Some English-speaking theologians play with the distinction between "immediate" and "mediate." There are, in other words, times in which we realize our hope and respond to our faith in a direct way with nothing between us as individual entities and God. There are other times when we must accept the mediation of the life in which we have been put.

9. This latter aspect of our hope has been strongly urged both by some European theologians (see J. Moltman, *Theology of Hope,* 1976) and at Vatican II. The *Pastoral Constitution on the Church in the*

Modern World begins with the words: "The joy and hope, the grief and anguish of the men of our time, especially of those who are poor or afflicted in any way, are the joy and hope, the grief and anguish of the followers of Christ as well. Nothing that is genuinely human fails to find an echo in their hearts, for theirs is a community composed of men, of men who, united in Christ and guided by the Holy Spirit, press onward toward the kingdom of the Father and are bearers of a message of salvation intended for all men" (*Gaudium et spes,* n. 1).

10. The notion that spirituality is concerned with a private relationship between a particular individual and God is a narrow and relatively modern notion, not popular until the seventeenth century. I would accept Josef Sudbrack's argument that the biblical and historical development of Christian spirituality should be taken to mean "the personal assimilation of the salvific mission of Christ by each Christian" ("Spirituality," *Encyclopedia of Theology,* pp. 1623ff). In other words, the same phenomenon is unfolding in the world community, hopefully through the Church, as is unfolding in the individual. I would further agree that a spirituality directed exclusively toward the interior life is simply a post-Reformation historical reaction. In the United States at least, these practices degenerated into a devotionalism which reached its furthest development in the 1950's. We are now in a new, as yet undefined, dimension which will no longer make it possible to confine spirituality to an interior life. This book, however, is not written in response to the changes of a new picture of spirituality. Rather this is a response to the practical void created when seventeenth century attitudes floundered and passed out of the picture. The result led to a lack of interior formation. Perhaps all suggestions at this time are only provisional until a new concept of spirituality emerges. Hopefully, contemporary contributions can contribute to that unfolding.

11. Or "koinonia."

12. Or "diacona."

13. This trend has been furthered by a growing number of theologians, one of the most noticeable being Louis Boyer, who published his *History of Christian Spirituality* (New York: Seabury Press), in the 1960's. Boyer was a French priest coming from a Protestant background—a professor of spiritual theology at the Institut Catholique, and a priest of the Oratory in Paris. He clearly maintains that dogmatic theology is interrelated with spirituality and that spirituality presupposes certain beliefs. However, he makes a distinction that "instead of studying or describing the objects of a belief, as it were in the abstract, it [spirituality] studies the reaction which these objects arouse in the religious consciousness." Boyer cautiously opens the door to spiritual les-

sons which can be learned from the human sciences. The process moved along much more rapidly after Vatican II with the growing popularity of "theological anthropology."

Chapter 3

1. Probably everything said here is reversed for people who are left-handed.

2. A non-technical work for those generally interested would be Bob Samples, *The Metaphoric Mind: A Celebration of Creative Consciousness* (Reading, Mass: Addison-Wesley Publishing Co., 1976).

3. An approach to education which recognizes brain hemisphere specialization can be found in such books as John Miller, *The Compassionate Teacher: How to Teach and Learn with Your Whole Self* (Englewood Cliffs, N.J.: Prentice-Hall, 1981).

4. These linkages have been severed at times for surgical reasons. The most common situation has to do with epilepsy patients. The results have sometimes been dramatic and constructive.

5. Research by Norman Geschwind at Harvard and other endocrine specialists may suggest a link between an unusual pre-birth excess of the hormone testosterone and an abnormal growth in the left hemisphere, possibly contributing to learning disabilities.

6. See Joseph Bogen, *Some Educational Implications of Hemispheric Specialization in the Human Brain* (Englewood Cliffs, N.J.: Prentice-Hall, 1977), p. 135.

7. *The Tao: The Sacred Way,* ed. by Tolbert McCarroll (New York: Crossroad, 1982), p. 5.

8. *Ibid.,* p. 101.

9. See Roland Murphy, O. Carm., *Wisdom Literature* (Grand Rapids: Wm. B. Eerdmans, 1981), and Pheme Perkins, *Hearing the Parables of Jesus* (New York: Paulist Press, 1981).

10. Edward Schillebeeckx, O.P., *Jesus: An Experiment in Christology* (New York: The Seabury Press, 1979), p. 626.

11. Jan Lambrecht, S.J., *Once More Astonished: The Parables of Jesus* (New York: Crossroad, 1981), p. 4.

12. Of course, there is a contrary school of thought, supported by the author of Mark at least, that the parables are intentionally obscure writings which are made perfectly clear to the initiated. This corresponds to the occult practice of the mystery religions of Jesus' time.

13. Pheme Perkins, *Hearing the Parables of Jesus* (New York: Paulist Press, 1981), pp. 35ff.

14. This is generally considered to come from the ancient material known as the "Q" source.

15. *The Anchor Bible: Matthew,* Vol. 26, trans. by W. F. Albright and C. S. Mann (Garden City, New York: Doubleday and Company, 1971), pp. 135ff.

Chapter 4

1. Clarence Thompson, "Right-Brain Religious Education," *National Catholic Reporter,* March 26, 1982.

2. James M. Clark, *Meister Eckhart: An Introduction to the Study of His Works with an Anthology of His Sermons* (Edinburgh: Thomas Nelson & Sons, Ltd., 1957), p. 147, Sermon 4.

3. Dean R. Hoge, *Converts, Dropouts and Returnees: A Study of Religious Change Among Catholics,* for the United States Catholic Conference, Washington, D.C. (New York: The Pilgrim Press, 1981), p. 97.

4. Ronald Goldman, *Religious Thinking from Childhood to Adolescence* (London: Routledge and Kegan Paul, 1964).

5. John H. Westerhoff, III, *Will Our Children Have Faith?* (New York: The Seabury Press, 1976), p. 51.

6. Bob Samples, *The Metaphoric Mind: A Celebration of Creative Consciousness* (Reading, Mass: Addison-Wesley Publishing Co., 1976), p. 58.

7. Quoted from a thirteenth century text, "Le Grand Propriétaire de toutes choses," quoted in Philippe Ariès, *Centuries of Childhood: A Social History of Family Life* (New York: Vintage Books, 1962), p. 21.

8. Erik H. Erikson, *Childhood and Society,* 2nd ed. (New York: W. W. Norton & Company, 1963).

9. *Sharing the Light of Faith* (Washington, D.C.: United States Catholic Conference, 1979).

10. *Ibid.,* para. 177ff.

11. *Ibid.,* para. 175.

Chapter 5

1. Morton T. Kelsey, *The Other Side of Silence: A Guide to Christian Meditation* (New York: Paulist Press, 1976), p. 21.

2. Isabel Briggs-Meyers with Peter B. Meyers, *Gifts Differing* (Palo Alto: Consulting Psychologists Press, Inc., 1980), p. 193.

3. *Ibid.,* p. 194.

4. *Ibid.*

5. Rudolf Dreikurs, M.D. (with Vicki Soltz, R.N.), *Children: The Challenge* (New York: Hawthorn Books, 1964).

6. Abraham H. Maslow, *Religions, Values and Peak Experiences* (Columbus: Ohio State University Press, 1964).

7. *Ibid.,* p. 42.

8. *Ibid.,* p. 43.

9. Abraham H. Maslow, *Motivation and Personality,* 2nd ed. (New York: Harper and Row, 1970), p. 163.

10. *Ibid.,* p. 164.

11. Abraham H. Maslow, *The Farthest Reaches of Human Nature* (New York: The Viking Press, 1971), p. 172.

12. Gordon W. Allport, *The Individual and His Religion: A Psychological Interpretation* (New York: Macmillan Publishing Company, 1950).

13. *Ibid.,* Ch. 2, pp. 31–57.

14. J. Piaget, *The Language and Thought of the Child* (New York: Harcourt Brace and Co., 1932).

15. Allport, *op. cit.,* p. 35.

Chapter 6

1. Rabindranath Tagore, *The Religion of Man* (Boston: Beacon Press, 1961), p. 198. The lectures were originally given at Oxford in 1930.

2. *Ibid.,* p. 200.

3. See Jean Leclercq, *Monks and Love in Twelfth-Century France: Psycho-Historical Essays* (Oxford: Oxford University Press, 1979).

4. See, for example, H. V. Gunther, and L. S. Kawamura, *Mind and Psychology* (Berkeley: Dharma Publishing, 1975).

5. James Schultz, "Stages on the Spiritual Path: A Buddhist Perspective," in *The Journal of Transpersonal Psychology,* Vol. 7, No. 1, 1975, p. 18.

6. Chogyam Trungpa, as told to Esme Cramer Roberts, *Born in Tibet* (Baltimore: Penguin Books, 1971). Originally published in England in 1966.

7. *Ibid.,* pp. 46–47.

8. *Ibid.,* p. 48.

9. *Ibid.,* p. 49.

10. *Ibid.,* p. 50.

11. *Ibid.,* p. 51.

Chapter 7

1. *Sharing the Light of Faith* (Washington, D.C.: United States Catholic Conference, 1979), para. 177.

Chapter 8

1. *The Tao: The Sacred Way,* ed. by Tolbert McCarroll (New York: Crossroad, 1982), Chapter 48, p. 101.

2. Psalm 45(46). This phrase is found in many religious traditions other than Judaeo-Christian.

3. This position was held by some medieval spiritual guides. See, for example, Francisco de Osuna, *The Third Spiritual Alphabet* (New York: Paulist Press, 1981).

4. Chogyam Trungpa, *Cutting Through Spiritual Materialism* (Berkeley: Shambhala, 1973).

Chapter 9

1. Rudolph Otto, *The Idea of the Holy* (New York: Oxford University Press, 1923).

2. See Frank Waters, *Book of the Hopi* (Conversations with Oswald White Bear Fredericks) (New York: Viking Press, 1963), p. 177.

3. *Ibid.,* p. 186 for a description of such an occurrence.

4. Mt 4:1–11; Mk 1:12–13; Lk 22:41–46.

5. Mt 26:36–46; Mk 14:32–42; Lk 22:41–46.

6. See John Miller, *The Compassionate Teacher* (Englewood Cliffs: Prentice-Hall, 1981). A generally fine chapter on "Silence" (pp. 63–93) should be of practical assistance to many parents and teachers. It also contains references to many of the other works available.

Chapter 10

1. John Courtney Murray, "The Return to Tribalism," in *The Catholic Mind,* LX, January 1962, p. 6. From an address to the John A. Ryan Forum and Adult Education Center on April 14, 1961.

2. Although not so universal as Sigmund Freud and some of his followers have proclaimed.

3. Alfred Adler, *Superiority and Social Interests: A Collection of Later Writings,* ed. by Heinz L. Ansbacher and Rowena Ansbacher (Evanston: Northwestern University Press, 1964), p. 98.

4. Michael Pennock, "Teaching Christian Morality!" in *Teaching Religion in the 80's,* ed. by Sister Vincenze Gagliostro, S.S.N.D. (Dayton: Pflaum Press, 1979), p. 8.

5. It would be inaccurate to indicate that none of early normative training has any effect in later life. The "I was taught that was wrong" is a phrase that has not entirely passed out of adolescent speech. Also, there is a much better clarification of the norms being used. There now is as much emphasis on the concepts in the Sermon on the Mount as with the Ten Commandments. Today there is much

more theological sophistication and the formation of conscience increasingly relies upon reflection intertwining personal experience with secular knowledge and the total lore of our Christian tradition.

With the teenager there does begin to develop the concept of individual ethical choice. Most often that freedom is seen as an opportunity of escaping from the restrictions imposed in earlier times, including normative morality. An interesting double phenomenon often develops. First, on the one hand the teenager's posture to the world is a rejection of all moral authority (although it may be modified a bit when talking to respected adults). As a result, any codes of conduct based upon norms and authority tend to be thrown out, no matter how useful they might be. On the other hand, there is a different posture toward peers with whom the teenager is developing a new sense of the world. Here we often hear the need for some regulating of this absolute freedom. Otherwise, "people" (meaning the teenager postulating the position) can get hurt. However, even at this point the "You ought not to do this because" type of reasoning is pretty well rejected. The tendency is more toward John Dewey's admonition: "Act as to increase the meaning of present existence." The action can be purely hedonistic, or it can be a reasoned choosing between known alternatives. The best that can be hoped for in the more difficult times of adolescence would be a sort of vague sense of ethical conduct based on interdependence of one young person to another, and perhaps even to the rest of the world. If a particular experience creates a greater sense of trust, appreciation for others, increases the capacity of people to work together or increases an individual's sense of himself or herself, of self-respect, or whatever other values are important at the particular age when one happens to be a teenager, then an action is seen as being positive. In the application of ethics to sexual experimentation, these approaches are actually put into rather formal presentations by many counselors as a way of suggesting a palatable standard which is not entirely pleasure oriented.

Twenty years ago I wrote a discussion guide for teenagers which was more or less based upon this purely interpersonal approach. I would do it differently today. The difficulty is that we are not teenagers for long and there is another phase of life. If during adolescence we tend to restrict our sense of "existence" to the interpersonal, we enter adulthood with a very narrow view. It is important to somehow keep the religious and spiritual aspects of our heritage alive even during this adolescent time of great doubt and conflict.

6. Carl R. Rogers, *On Becoming a Person: A Therapist's View of Psychotherapy* (Boston: Houghton-Mifflin Co., 1961), pp. 164–165.

7. *Ibid.,* p. 166.

8. Martin Buber, *I and Thou* (New York: Charles Scribner & Sons, 1970).

9. *Ibid.,* p. 126.

Chapter 11

1. *The Tao: The Sacred Way,* ed. by Tolbert McCarroll (New York: Crossroad, 1982), Chapter 25, p. 53.

2. This may be reading too much into the verse which may simply be denouncing emperors or other men made gods.

3. Karl Rahner, "Prayer," in *Encyclopedia of Theology: The Concise Sacramentum Mundi* (New York: Crossroad, 1982), pp. 1268ff.

4. James Hennesey, S.J., *American Catholics* (New York: Oxford University Press, 1981), p. 288.

5. For a more detailed description of lectio divina see: A Monk of the Abbey of New Clairvaux, *But Don't You Belong to Me?* (Ramsey, N.J.: Paulist Press, 1979), or Augustine Roberts, *Centered on Christ* (Stillwater, Mass.: St. Bede's Publications, 1977).

Chapter 12

1. This is usually found either as Chapter 13 of the Book of Daniel (in some places Chapter 1) or in the apocryphal section under the "Book (or History) of Susanna."

2. Avery Dulles, S.J., *A Church To Believe In* (New York: Crossroad, 1982), p. 37.

3. What is possible is to include in the confirmation process, although outside the realm of this book, what is usually called "moral development." This might more accurately be described in this country as the evolution from moral (that is, making decisions relying upon norms) judgments to an ethical sensitivity or awareness which links behavior to a more mature and all-inclusive response to life. This area of concern has been much more seriously developed in Europe than here. The contributions of Christiane Brusselmans and other Europeans can help us. The major agenda is to encourage the child to grow from an ego-centered attitude into a more altruistically oriented person. The child usually has a period of relying upon "do and don't," "reward and punishment," acting out of concern for external authority, which must be sensitively developed into a more internalized approach that accepts extenuating and intenuating circumstances and places a heavier reliance upon motives than upon objective acts.

Interestingly enough, the Native American cultures which have so flavored the discusson of this step had little interest in moral decision-making. It did not play a significant role in the religious upbringing of the child. This is probably because of the uniform code of behavior which was such a strong part of the culture that it simply limited a person's options. With increased personal freedom, as in our own society, there comes the need for greater moral sensitivity and responsibility.

4. Helder Camara, *Spiral of Violence* (London: Sheed and Ward, 1971), p. 80.

5. Bernard Häring, *Free and Faithful in Christ,* Vol. 3 (New York: Crossroad Publishing Co., 1981), pp. 216–217.

6. The last few paragraphs are an adaptation of a meditation from my *Notes from the Song of Life* (Millbrae: Celestial Arts, 1977, 1982), XII, "Pain," pp. 61–62.

Chapter 13

1. Thomas Merton, *The Climate of Monastic Prayer* (Spencer: Cistercian Publications, 1969), p. 57.

2. Morton T. Kelsey, *Dreams: The Dark Speech of the Spirit* (Garden City: Doubleday, 1968). See also his popular book, *Dreams: A Way To Listen to God* (New York: Paulist Press, 1978).

3. The aspect of Jungian theory most popular in Christian circles today has to do with the complex symbolization process and archetypes which do not really relate to the use of dreams as presented here.

4. Frederick S. Perls, *Gestalt Therapy Verbatim* (Lafayette: Real People Press, 1969).

5. E. L. Hartmann, "The D-State: A Review and Discussion on the Physiological State Concomitant with Dreaming," *The International Journal of Psychiatry* 2, 1966, pp. 11–31.

6. Kilton Stewart, "Culture and Personality in Two Primitive Groups," *Complex,* Winter 1953–1954, p. 20.

7. Kilton Stewart, "Dream Theory in Malaya," N. Charles Tart, ed., *Altered States of Consciousness* (New York: John Wiley and Sons, 1969).

Chapter 14

1. Karl Rahner, *Concern for the Church* (New York: Crossroad, 1981), p. 85.

2. *Ibid.,* pp. 143–153.

3. *Ibid.,* p. 145.

4. *Ibid.,* p. 147.

5. *Ibid.,* p. 148.

6. *Ibid.,* p. 149.

7. *Ibid.,* p. 129.

8. *Ibid.,* p. 152.

9. *Ibid.,* p. 153.

10. *Ibid.,* p. 152.

11. *Ibid.,* p. 153.

12. Joseph Gelineau, *The Liturgy Today and Tomorrow* (New York: Paulist Press, 1979), p. 113.

Chapter 15

1. John H. Westerhoff III, *Will Our Children Have Faith?* (New York: Seabury, 1976), p. 96.

2. John A. T. Robinson, *The Roots of a Radical* (New York: Crossroad, 1981), p. 96.

3. See Chapter 14 and also Karl Rahner's *Concern for the Church* (New York: Crossroad, 1982).

4. Arnold Toynbee, *Experiences* (New York: Oxford University Press, 1969), pp. 324–325.

5. To adapt an image of Yves Congar.

6. Avery Dulles, S.J., from a sermon at the National Shrine of the Immaculate Conception, Washington, D.C., Jan. 22, 1966 (quoted in *Catholic Mind* 64, May 1966, pp. 31–32).

7. Bernard Lonergan, *Methods in Theology* (New York: Seabury, 1972), p. 241.

Appendix A

1. Matsuo Basho (tr. Nobuyuki Yuasa), *The Narrow Road to the Deep North and Other Travel Sketches* (Baltimore: Penguin Books, 1966), from the translator's introduction, p. 33.

Appendix B

1. Dean R. Hoge, *Converts, Dropouts, Returnees* (New York: Pilgrim Press, 1981), p. 92.

2. Bob Samples, *The Metaphoric Mind: A Celebration of Creative Consciousness* (Reading: Addison-Wesley, 1981), pp. 59–60.

3. See George B. Leonard, *Education and Ecstasy* (New York: Delacorte Press, 1968), pp. 3ff.

4. Richard McBrien, *Catholicism* (Oak Grove: Winston Press, Study Edition, 1981), p. 972.

5. Leonard, *op. cit.,* p. 13.

6. John H. Westerhoff III, *Will Our Children Have Faith?* (New

York: Seabury, 1976). See especially Chapter 3, "In Search of Community," pp. 51ff.

7. Ronald Goldman, *Readiness for Religion: The Basis for Developmental Religious Education* (New York: Seabury, 1965).

8. *National Catechetical Directory* (Washington, D.C.: United States Catholic Conference, 1979), pp. 113–114.

9. Bernard Häring, *The Law of Christ* (Ramsey, N.J.: Newman Press, 1966), p. 139.

10. *Ibid.,* p. 143.

INDEX